Eastern Christianity

THE BYZANTINE TRADITION

Eastern Christianity
THE BYZANTINE TRADITION

LAWRENCE CROSS

E. J. DWYER
Sydney • Philadelphia

This edition published 1988 by
E.J. Dwyer Pty Ltd
Unit 3, 32-72 Alice Street
Newtown NSW 2042
Australia

E.J. Dwyer Pty Ltd
2772 Country Club Road
Philadelphia PA 19131
U.S.A.

Biblical quotations are taken from *The Jerusalem Bible*, published by Darton,
Longman & Todd Limited, London, 1966, and are used with their permission.

Nihil Obstat: Peter R. Cross M.A.(Oxon), S.T.D.
          Diocesan Censor

Imprimatur: Peter J. Connors D.C.L.
          Vicar General
          Archdiocese of Melbourne
          5 March, 1986

The Nihil Obstat and Imprimatur are official declarations that a book
or pamphlet is free of doctrinal or moral error. No implication is
contained therein that those who have granted the Nihil Obstat and
Imprimatur agree with the contents, opinions or statements expressed.

National Library of Australia
Cataloguing-in-Publication data

Cross, Lawrence.
   Eastern Christianity.

   Bibliography.
   ISBN 0 85574 148 1.

   1. Eastern churches.   2. Orthodox Eastern Church —
History.   3. Byzantine Empire — Civilization.
   I. Title.
281′.5

Library of Congress Cataloguing-in-Publication data

Cross, Lawrence, 1943—
   Eastern Christianity: the Byzantine tradition/Lawrence Cross.
      p.   cm.
   Bibliography: p.
   ISBN 0-85574-148-1
   1. Orthodox Eastern Church.   I. Title.
BX320.2.C76   1988
281.9 — dc19   88-22894
                                                    CIP

Typeset in Hong Kong by Setrite Typesetters Limited
Printed in Australia by Southwood Press Pty Limited, Marrickville

for
Nicholas David

Ἴδε ἡ μήτηρ σου.

ACKNOWLEDGMENT

I wish to thank Andrew Quinlan, Diane Walsh, Father Peter Knowles and Archimandrite George Branch for their invaluable ideas, critical appraisals and personal support. I would have lost heart without them.

I also wish to thank Sidgwick & Jackson Limited for permission to reproduce the illustration on page 83 by Takis Zervoulakos, from the book *Athos, The Holy Mountain* by Philip Sherrard, published by Sidgwick & Jackson Limited.

Contents

Introduction   1

Chapter One
Historical Outlines   5

    Origins   6
    Differentiation   9
    Estrangement   12
    Schism   18

Chapter Two
The Byzantine Theological View   25

    Gospel, Culture and Byzantium   26
    Trinity and Incarnation   29
    The Mystery of the Church   33
    The Bishop in the Church   40
    Holy Tradition   47
    The *Laos*, People of God   49

Chapter Three
The Sacramental Mysteries   55

    An Approach to the Sacraments   56
    Eucharist   58
    Marriage   60
    Penance   62
    Fast and Feast   65

Chapter Four
Tradition in Life   69

    Earth Made Heaven   70
    The Worshipper in the Church   74
    Monasticism   81
    Icons   86
    The Jesus Prayer   90

Chapter Five
Eastern Christianity, Today and Tomorrow   95

    The Orthodox Church Today   96
    Eastern Rite Catholics   98
    Toward Reunion   99
    Beginning to Understand   103

Conclusion   107

Appendixes
1: Genealogy of the Christian Liturgies   110
2: Further Reading   111

References   113

Introduction

The purpose of this work is to provide interested Christians with an introduction to Eastern Christianity and to assist the reader to come as close to an understanding of the Eastern Christian believer as possible. In countries such as the United States, Canada, Australia and, to a lesser extent, the United Kingdom, this understanding is particularly important, since Eastern Christians of one sort or another now account for a significant part of the population. An almost unique opportunity exists in the new lands for Western and Eastern Christians to arrive at an understanding which the homelands of Europe did not so readily provide.

Understanding cannot be obtained without effort. The interested reader should be prepared to read something of the history of the Christian East and to give some attention to its theology. One cannot understand the feelings of those who are being approached without some history. One cannot penetrate their self-understanding without some knowledge of their theological view. This book is an invitation to begin to both feel and see the Eastern Christian world view.

This book is about Eastern Christians, but the terms that it will use for them will alter. When you read Eastern Orthodox Christians, the Orthodox, Byzantine Christians or Byzantine Christianity, remember that for our purposes these terms are interchangeable and mean much the same thing. Most Eastern Europeans are Christians in the Eastern tradition of Christianity, which includes, to name a few by way of introduction, almost all Greeks, Russians, Bulgarians, Macedonians, Serbs, Rumanians, Slavic Macedonians, Byelorussians and Ukrainians, and some Arabs, Poles, Finns and Albanians. Some knowledge of them is important, since families from this tradition may now be our neighbors with children at school with our children.

In the past and up to the present there are grave and deep misunderstandings and prejudices existing between the Western and Eastern churches. Father I. Dalmais, writing in the journal *Istina* in 1961, illustrates the sort of penalty that Western Christians paid for the loss of communion with the Eastern churches. He believes that had the Roman church been still in communion with the East, it may not have suffered Christendom's second disaster, the Reformation. Orthodoxy, or the Eastern tradition of Catholicism, may very well have contained many of the answers sought by those who became Protestant reformers. The experience of Orthodoxy may well have decisively tempered the problems and conflicts which beset the West in the late Middle Ages and early modern period. In short, the West may have had more resources with which to deal with dissent if East and West were living in communion. In the same way, Orthodoxy may have

The Transfiguration (Metamorphosis), a twelfth-century icon from the Monastery of St. Katherine, Mount Sinai. As heavenly light, the divine glory shines out from the person of Jesus.

been less a prey to despotism and countless other sufferings if she had access to some of the strengths of the West. This may well be still true of both churches today.

This may be a little confusing for someone who as yet knows little about Eastern Orthodox Christians. Who are the Orthodox? The shortest answer is that they are the other side of the Catholic soul. The reverse is also true. The Catholics are the other side of the Orthodox soul. This may seem to be no more than an empty assertion at this stage, but the purpose of this book is to show that this is indeed the case. If it is right to say that the separation of the Roman and Orthodox churches was the greatest and saddest disaster ever to befall mankind, then the rediscovery and restoration of communion between the churches will also be the church's happiest day since Pentecost. This little book is written in the certain belief that this happiest of days will one day dawn. All Christians of the Catholic, Protestant and Orthodox traditions can participate, if they do no more than widen their knowledge and enlarge their sympathies for each other.

CHAPTER ONE

Historical Outlines

ORIGINS

In the past there was unity between what was to become the Catholic and the Orthodox churches, but if we are to understand anything of their relationship, we must look at the outlines of their history at least. This is rather like getting to know a long-lost relative's background and what it means for that person. It helps one to rediscover, love and serve that relative properly in the present, as well as to face the future together. As with man and man, so it is with the churches. In this case it leads Catholics to look again at their own past and present, perhaps with new eyes. If our object is to enlarge our sympathies and our experience of Eastern Orthodox Christians, an historical perspective is essential.

The new life of Jesus Christ was carried by his apostles beyond the cultural and racial limits of Judaism into the larger world of the Gentiles. In the apostolic era up to the fifth century this larger world was mostly the dominant culture of the Greco–Roman world and empire. The Roman Empire was the westernmost empire of the two great powers west of India. The other was Persia. The Roman world was founded upon the original scattering of Greek cities which the Romans had taken over in their rise to power in the Mediterranean region. These cities, united by efficient communications, ruled by a central government and protected by the legions, were the places in which the apostles and disciples preached Christ, first to the Jews, then to the pagans.

The Greco–Roman world at its widest extent in the second century stretched from the borders of Wales in Britain to the town of Dura Europus on the Euphrates. It was ruled from Rome by Caesar, the lord of the world. It was mostly in Caesar's world that the apostles preached and ministered Christ. For some 249 years the church of Jesus Christ was persecuted by Caesar and his ministers in public, and challenged from within by the odd and bewildering religious leanings of the men and women of the Greco–Roman world. It is important to know something about this world in order to make sense of later developments and because it was the crucible of Christianity.

The Greco–Roman world was truly cosmopolitan. Men and women from far-flung parts could move about in it without fear of cultural dislocation or disorientation. The dominant languages were commercial Greek (the language of the New Testament), which most people spoke as well as their regional tongues, and Latin (the language of law and administration), which was more common in the western regions of the Empire. The most cultivated, artistic and literary center was Alexandria in Egypt, while Rome was usually the administrative and political capital until the Empire's center of gravity began to alter after the second century. What was to become Constantinople and New Rome was still the sleepy town of Byzantium until the capital was moved there in the fourth century.

This world was cosmopolitan and so was the Christian church. The second-century figure of St. Irenaeus illustrates this. From Smyrna in Asia Minor, he learned the faith from St. Polycarp, a disciple of St. John. His language was Greek and his environment Middle Eastern, yet he became the bishop of the church of Lyons in what is now central France. In those days it was in the province of Trans-Alpine Gaul. Up to the opening of the fourth century it is almost meaningless to talk of Eastern and Western Christians. The church consisted of Christians gathered around their bishops in the towns and cities of the Roman world, enduring both persecution from the State and classical paganism, and attempts at undermining the Christian faith by various mystery cults and doctrinally derailed Christians who flourished in the dilettantish religious world of the late Roman Empire.

There were as yet no Eastern, Western or Oriental churches. Rather, there were great indicative figures among the fathers and writers of the early church who began to bring habits of mind and particular talents and insights, associated with particular regions of the Empire, into the service of the church and of Christ's truth.

In the West, where Latin, the law and a talent for administration predominated, a man like Tertullian, a passionate North African lawyer and Christian controversialist, summoned words and concepts from his legal background for use in his theology, which was addressed to the disputes of the day that involved Christians living in the western regions. *Meritum, satisfacere* and *culpa* (merit, satisfaction and fault) show the first glimmerings of the rather juridical way in which Christians of the West will tend to speak of salvation, grace and reconciliation.

In Alexandria, the cultural center of Roman Hellenism and the greatest city in the Middle Eastern Roman world, there arose another figure, Origen, who without doubt was the formative genius of the early church. His exposition of the Scriptures and his defense of the Christian faith led him, reluctantly at first, to forge links between the Christian faith and useful philosophical concepts of the Greeks. Like that of Tertullian, Origen's work was not without fault. But, when he wrote that 'from him [Jesus] began the union of the divine with the human nature, so that the human, by communion with the divine, might rise to be divine, not in Jesus alone, but in all who believe and enter upon the life that Jesus taught,'[1] he sounded the theme that was to be dominant in the Eastern Christian view of salvation, grace and reconciliation.

The Oriental churches who in 451 were to break off communion with the Latins and the Greeks (for want of better terms at this stage when the church was visibly one) already held and continued to hold to a theological scheme similar in almost all points to the Middle Eastern (Greek) school of theology initiated by Origen. They broke communion over a doctrinal dispute involving the relationship of the divine and human natures of Jesus. Fortunately this did not happen until after they had made their own what Pope John XXIII described as 'the entire later doctrinal edifice of theology in the East and West [which] rests on the mighty shoulders of St. Basil, St. Gregory Nazianzus and their fellows.' Even on the one matter where they did dissent from the Latin West and the Greek East in the Council of Chalcedon in 451, the relationship of the divine and human in Christ, practical correctness of belief was restored in a quite short time. Unfortunately politics and other deep grievances made the way back to reunion impossible. The first serious division in Christ's church had occurred and lasts to our own day.[2]

It was meaningless to talk of Eastern and Western churches in the time of Tertullian or Origen, but by the fourth and fifth centuries St. Augustine, bishop of Hippo in North Africa (in some ways the most Latin province of all), had produced the first great synthesis of the faith in a Western context, responding to the problems and lessons in the experience of Western Christians. A distinctly Western theology had finally arrived, written by a man who knew little Greek. The same is true of the East. From the painful controversies about the doctrine of the Holy Trinity and the equally bitter struggles in Christology, the true understanding of Jesus Christ, which Origen and other early fathers had begun, was completed and corrected in the labors of St. Basil, St. Gregory of Nyssa and St. Gregory Nazianzus. The main lines of the distinctive nature of Eastern Christian approaches to theology had finally been established.

In both East and West, regional experiences conditioned the work. Western Christians were certainly touched by the grave matters concerning the Holy Trinity and the person of Jesus Christ, but they were mostly preoccupied with either disciplinary or practical problems. The one great speculative issue which occupied St. Augustine even exhibited this more practical bent. In his controversy with Pelagius[3] (a British monk who taught that man was morally perfectible by his own efforts and thus capable of meriting salvation by his own strivings), Augustine was forced to meet him on topics such as sin, redemption, the nature of grace, free will, predestination and the nature of the church.

In the Middle Eastern Roman world, which can now be seen as clearly Greek in its habits of mind and where understanding of the Latin language was becoming something of a rarity, the Cappadocian fathers (as St. Basil and his friends were called) were forced to deal with more speculative and mystical matters, such as the divinity of the Holy Spirit, the true manhood and divinity of Jesus, and the person of Christ as the source of Christian holiness.

By the fourth and fifth centuries one can talk about clearly Western and the Eastern churches, but they are still the one, holy, catholic and apostolic church, and will remain in unity for another five or so centuries. It was in these next centuries that the causes of the severing of visible communion (schism) took shape, a division which took place somewhere between 1054 and the early thirteenth century.

The three chief divisions of the Catholic church have a common birth and childhood in the Greco–Roman world. They are like triplets who learned common tastes and mannerisms which persist to this day, although more personal styles have developed in their later lives. Even so, they bear the tell-tale mannerisms which point them out as blood relatives. Although these children of the one Father left each other at different times, none of them has a claim to greater antiquity than any other. None is any more apostolic than another. Nor can any one of them claim that only its particular development and differentiation (from their common childhood to differentiated adulthood) is the only proper and universal form of differentiation.

The Western Catholic, Eastern Orthodox and Oriental churches are certainly not identical triplets, but they do have the same fundamental rights as children of the one Father. As the body of his Christ they are manifestly sustained by the same Holy Spirit, the source of all spiritual reality, whose presence, through the guarantee of Jesus, cannot be lost to them, nor has it been in what is now almost two thousand years of Christian life.

DIFFERENTIATION

From 313 to 640, the Roman world and the Christian church experienced changes and developments so deep and extensive that they could not have even been dreamed of by men in the closing years of the third century. In this short space of three hundred years, the political, economic and social fabric of Roman Europe was profoundly altered both from within and by external pressures. The church itself inevitably underwent current change along with the world. In these years the three Catholic styles of church began to emerge more distinctly. Based upon a pre-existent foundation of language, culture and geography, the development of styles was hastened.

The crucial event which influenced all of the churches at the opening of the fourth century was the unexpected conversion of the Emperor Constantine to the Christian faith. The responses of the Eastern and Western spheres of church life were quite distinctive. The Greek East was more comfortable with the Emperor's conversion than was the Latin West. The Oriental sphere of church life welcomed Caesar's conversion even less enthusiastically, since for many of these Christians it meant only more Greek domination, except that now it was under a Christian Caesar.[4]

In so short a space we can only generalize and paint the larger historical scene with a very big brush but we must emphasize just how difficult and challenging the years 313 to 640 were for both the churches and the Roman world. These years encompassed the period from Constantine's conversion in 313 to the triumph in 640 of Islam in the eastern and northern African provinces of the Roman world. In the West the conversion of the Empire was less important than the reaction to the ending of persecution. While persecution put great pressure on the church, its abrupt cessation was also quite traumatic. This was the case for many Christians in the Western sphere. Many of them got something like spiritual diver's bends. Refusing to adjust, they sought to perpetuate the atmosphere of the persecuted church by opposing both the State and the Catholic church with an alternative movement known as Donatism, after its most talented organizer, the North African cleric Donatus.

The Donatist controversy shows us the sorts of issues that Western Christians were likely to be passionate about. The West tended to concern itself with problems of church order, discipline, moral issues, jurisdiction and government, whereas the Greek East wrestled with heresies which threatened the revealed truth about God, the Holy Trinity and the natures of Christ. It is curious that when the West did have its own serious doctrinal controversy in the fifth century, it was a heresy which taught error about the nature of man, saving grace and the nature of the redemption. At the risk of an enormous generalization, the Western and Eastern casts of mind are already discernible. The West is already tending to be more legalistic and realistically practical, giving much of its attention to the state of man before God. The East is more mystical and idealist, emphasizing the mystery of God.

From the very beginning, the genius of two civilizations, the Greek and the Latin, created and developed two currents of thought and two complementary manners of life in Christ. The period 313−640 sees these two approaches and styles taking shape. The experience of the Latin West and the Greek East in this period can only be described as most often quite horrendous. Neither East nor West had an easy time, though the East was to have more time than the West in which to work out the beautiful synthesis of faith and culture that is known as Byzantine civilization.

In the late fourth century Roman government in the West was in decline. Barbarian peoples now were very numerous within the Empire and there was a deep unease abroad. In the early fifth century the unthinkable happened. Barbarian people, known to history as the Vandals, invaded in force. Rome itself was sacked in 410. They swept on through Gaul and Spain and crossed even to Africa. Augustine died as Hippo prepared itself to endure a Vandal siege.

It seemed that the world was coming undone. In 476 the child emperor Romulus abdicated. The Empire came to an end in the West. The Christian emperor, in now far-off Constantinople, could do little to help. All was doubly confounded. Not only were the barbarians dissolving the West, but they were heretics as well. Their previous conversion to Arianism[5] gave an even sharper edge to their hostility. The bishops of the Roman towns and cities became almost the only focus for stability in what must have seemed like a world of nightmare. Facing enormous difficulties, the church set out to convert the barbarians to Catholicism. The turning point was the conversion of the leader of the one great barbarian tribe which was still pagan and which was also destined to dominate politically and militarily in Western Europe. The leader was Clovis, baptized in 496. His people were the Franks.

The churchmen of the Catholic Roman West finally turned the tide, but the practical task of evangelization became their chief concern. The Western churches were absorbed with the double task of converting and civilizing for another five hundred years, a task which further reinforced their practical bent. Absorption in this task, as well as the shocks and changes of this newer emerging world, made it almost impossible to pay much more than fleeting attention to their brothers in the Christian East, who were also fighting for their faith and their security on many fronts, including repelling the incursions of the forces of Islam and sending out missionaries to eastern Europe. The East however had one important advantage. The capital and the homelands were never overrun. Because of this, the life of Byzantium was more or less untouched by the wanderers, making it a continuous civilization.

ESTRANGEMENT

There is no period in ecumenical history quite so misunderstood and neglected as the years 500 to 1000 A.D. Touched by the anti-Christian spirit of much of post-eighteenth-century historical writings, historians have persisted in calling this period the Dark Ages. The title dismisses the Western church's struggle to convert and civilize the barbarians as beyond admiration, while it almost ignores the existence of Byzantium, which was the flowering of the Roman East into one of the most beautiful and fascinating cultures ever known. In the pages of the unsympathetic, the West is portrayed as crude and barbarous, the East as indolent and static. Both portrayals are unfair.

The church in the West was the guardian of what remained of civilization, such that civilization and church came to mean the same thing. The East was not all that different. The Roman world survived there precisely because the Christian faith gave it a new raison d'être, a new inner vision and strength. The saddest thing about this period was that circumstances dictated that the development of Christian civilization in the West and the East should take place separately. The enforced isolation of Eastern and Western churches in such a formative period created an ethos full of potential for misunderstanding when the churches came into renewed contact in the future. By the year 1000 there was already much about each church that was foreign to the other, such as the loss of common language, different liturgical customs and emphases, variations in church organization, different ways of responding to and living with the State, different missionary approaches and a whole host of variations in customs, such as fasting, prayer forms and devotions.

It may seem incongruous to people in the twentieth century to speak of almost complete isolation, but such was the case. In the early part of the period, Byzantium withdrew from the West to deal with its own barbarian menace, as well as to combat its almost constant enemy further to the East, the Persian Empire. The Byzantines had every intention of returning, as the Emperor Justinian's policy and activities in the sixth century clearly show, but events of the seventh century placed this beyond all possible

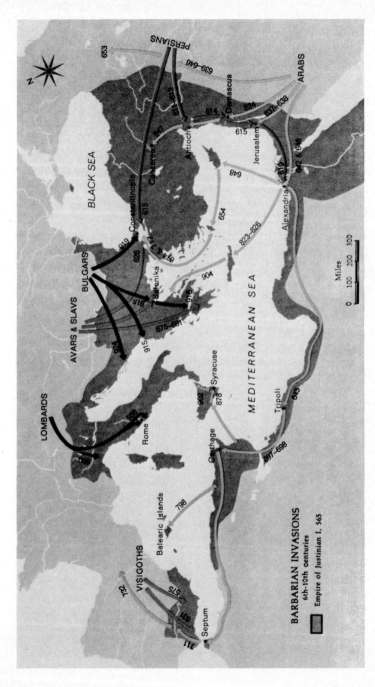

Map illustrating the barbarian invasions, sixth to tenth centuries.

hope. The rise of Islam, while it destroyed the Persians, engaged the attention of the Eastern Empire ever afterward, placing the final seal upon the withdrawal from the West.

By the Christmas of 800, the feast on which Pope Leo III crowned the Frankish king Charlemagne as emperor in the West, no emperor from Constantinople had visited Old Rome for three hundred years. A mere trickle of Byzantine art filtered westward, while the Greek language was almost forgotten. In their now quite discrete spheres, both churches produced a whole series of missionaries remarkable for their fervor and energy. Point for point they could match each other in their achievements. In the West, Franks and Germans, Anglo-Saxons and Visigoths were drawn into the Catholic fold, which included even the dreaded Norsemen by about the year 1000. The Byzantines worked among the Serbs, Rumanians, Georgians (evangelized by a nun, St. Nina) and Bulgars, finally drawing the Eastern Slavs of Rus into the faith in 988. Although almost parallel in their efforts, the missionary situation of West and East was not at all points the same.

While the Western missionaries had succeeded by 1000 in winning the barbarians to the faith, the task of civilizing them was by no means complete. Charlemagne's empire fragmented under less competent successors, making western Europe even more fiercely torn by constant feudal strife and vendetta. Though Christian, it was still a rough and dangerous society. Its greatest need was for a measure of stability and permanence. The church struggled to supply them, but it took time. The tide began to turn when men of intelligence began to make their career in the church, as the monasteries of the renewed Benedictine tradition founded new houses which were also centers of culture and permanence, as the church's measures against the violent began to have some effect (the Peace of God, and the Truce of God), and as the papacy began to regain some independence and prestige in the election of more worthy and capable popes. By the eleventh century a new power had clearly arrived in western Europe, a power for faith, culture and permanence. That power was the church, which represented the permanence of Divine Law in human society.

The East had a similar task, but the spirit in which it performed it, as well as the resources upon which it drew, indicates a quite different atmosphere prevailing in the East. Though beleaguered by enemies in the early part of the period 500−1000, the East saved the homelands of Greece, Asia Minor and the capital from destruction or occupation. It maintained itself as a continuously Greco−Roman civilization. The East retained not only the cul-

The interior of Hagia Sophia, Constantinople.

tural resources of the ancients, but the whole tradition of the fathers and the ecumenical councils. Its tradition of Scripture scholarship also remained undimmed. Nor did it lose its valued Christian institutions, most importantly the monastic heritage. All this produced the cultural and artistic synthesis of Byzantium's Christian vision. The opportunity to develop a sustained Christian way of life, mirrored in almost perfect buildings, deeply theological art and splendid liturgy, gave Byzantium's missionaries their most sustaining vision as well as their most powerful evangelical instrument. The use of the vernacular languages in both preaching and liturgy gave the newly converted lands immediate access to the chief sustenance of the Christian life. Byzantium realized very early that the realities of the faith were not to be encountered in concepts alone, but through signs and symbols intelligible to any worshipping congregation. Byzantine missionaries certainly preached and catechized, but the chief mark of the style of Eastern missionary activity was to establish a worshipping community, in which the celebration of the Holy Mysteries would speak for itself. For Eastern Christianity, it is the local eucharistic assembly which reveals and realizes the nature of the church. The Divine Liturgy transforms sinful men and women into the 'people of God,' thus revealing the reality of the church as the sacrament of the divine – human communion.

The way to the schism, which we will discuss in the next section, was prepared for in the so-called 'Dark Ages,' by folly and bigotry, but certainly by the development of different styles of church and mission. The energetic and practical West placed stability and permanence at a premium, focusing upon God's eternal design, of which the church was the visible expression. The West valued the permanence of Divine Law, which recalled the legal and corporate sense of the church foreshadowed in the writing of the earlier great thinkers of the West and which drew upon Roman legal traditions, language and forms. It is more than probable that the emergencies of the Dark Ages in the West reinforced its legal and practical tendencies. In the next period, 1000 to 1204, the churches will break off communion and the great schism will have occurred. But before we turn to that period, it is important to remember that when arguments break out over matters such as the authority of the Pope, the marriage of the clergy, the procession of the Holy Spirit, or whether clergy should shave, what the churches were really arguing about was something more fundamental, though hidden from them. It was the question of their conception of the church and their possession of it, which is to say, a difference of religious psychology.

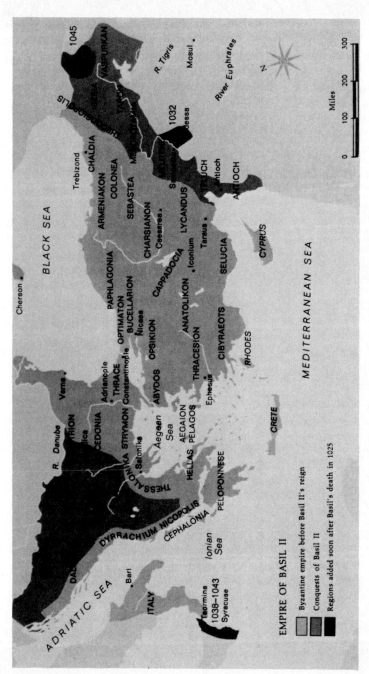

Map illustrating the Empire of Basil II, the Macedonian.

SCHISM

The actual schism between Old Rome and the Greek East took shape between the ninth and the thirteenth centuries. It is quite impossible to fix upon any one particular incident as the precise cause of the schism, rather the whole period from 863 to 1204 saw the fomenting of a spirit of schism; a poisonous and estranging process with which the churchmen colluded. One cannot exonerate either side, nor is it helpful to cast either party in the role of the 'good guys,' although finally one must have a greater sympathy for the Byzantines, since in the long term they suffered a much greater loss, including the weakening and the final collapse of their world as they had known it.

Popular history has customarily pointed to certain issues and specific incidents in its attempt to pinpoint the exact date of the schism of East and West. It has also been largely content to believe that these incidents are their own explanation. The so-called Photian Schism (863−869), which saw Pope Nicholas I and Patriarch Photius in conflict, and the celebrated year of 1054, which saw mutual excommunications exchanged between Patriarch Michael Cerularius and the papal legates to Constantinople, have often been singled out in this attempt. None of these, considered alone, can provide a satisfactory overview, or expose the source of the spirit of schism which continues to remain invisible.

The underlying cause, from which sprang so many of the incidents and irritations leading to actual and final schism, was the Roman legacy itself, a legacy inherited by both churches, although in different ways and with different emphases. The conversion of St. Constantine in 313, and with it the conversion of the Empire, was a mixed blessing. For the next thousand years and a little more, the Christian church accepted the advantages of association with the imperial authority. Both East and West accommodated the Roman idea into their customary ways of thinking and into their institutional and corporate life. There were great advantages but equally great risks and dangers. If by the Middle Ages we mean something like a new civilization in which the Roman idea became fused with Christianity and filled with the energies of new peoples, Chateaubriand was right when he said that 'Constantine engendered the middle ages.'

Both the Eastern and Western churches considered themselves Roman. Both were right to do so, but they claimed the heritage in different ways and expressed it variously. When Pope Leo III acted to recreate something of the Empire in the West in 800 by crowning Charlemagne, he was appealing to the Roman idea. He was not, however, intending to create a Basileus, an emperor and empire in the Byzantine mode and style. Although this simply was not possible within the West, the Greek East reacted in its own terms and saw the creation of an emperor in the West as a kind of secular schism, a kind of coup d'état, and worse still, by a barbarian and therefore contemptible. The Greeks remained unreconciled to these developments. The West long remained as lost Byzantine territories in their minds, a place now chaotic and formless. They never really understood the West's need to create order and stability in its own right, nor that the Western church, in creating new institutions and adapting others, was struggling 'to protect human society against fate and itself.'[6] A rigid policy on the part of the Roman church was not possible under these circumstances. The Byzantines disdained these developments in the West, failing to understand the spirit and circumstances that prevailed there. They remained very haughty indeed in the dealings they had with men whom they considered usurping barbarians.

It was probably impossible for them to respond otherwise, since Byzantium was in its golden age, while the West, within which the papacy contended, was a shabby and squalid thing in comparison. Nor was the papacy itself always free to act; nor was it always graced by worthy men. One writer has noted that while Byzantium was in its golden age, the papacy was largely in its age of lead. Many of its incumbents quite justifiably earned Byzantine contempt. Worse, in Byzantine eyes the West had perhaps made a fool of itself at the end of the ninth century. The empire of Charlemagne was in ruins, his world full of violence to the young and the unprotected, the towns depopulated, the monasteries burned and the rule of law in abeyance. What had become of this mock empire? Worse, the papacy itself seemed to have collapsed in a new wave of barbarism. The appearance was deceptive. Although in dire straits, the papacy and the church were still seen as the place in which the West's best hopes resided. Indeed, the papacy was to be the linchpin of the new society that was to emerge.

In the wreckage of the post-Carolingian West, the papacy slowly assumed and combined imperial and pontifical styles and ideology. Strong reforming figures such as Nicholas I and Gregory VII gave life and shape to this ideal, while the circumstances of life made it both possible and desirable. Western Christians longed for a strong papacy and men like Nicholas and Gregory gave that hope substance. It would be true to say that this longing for a strong papacy is a comment on the fundamental psychology of Western Christians. The role of the Holy See and appeals to Peter's primacy were not mere theory in the early medieval West. They were a life line which guaranteed the church, the church

St. Cyril and St. Methodios, apostles of the Slavs and symbols of unity.

which was the one voice that spoke of love and charity, the last light in the darkness, the sole embodiment of spiritual and intellectual values.

While the Byzantines never really understood the role of the papacy in the West and men's feelings toward it, the Western church failed to appreciate her sister in the East and the nature of her achievements. Roman civilization had been hard pressed, but it remained continuous in the East. It was the role of the church to suffuse that society with the values of the Gospel and the life of the Christian sacraments and to work at so deepening men's attachment to Christ in word and sacrament that Christianity became an intimate part of popular conscience and of imperial policy. This was not without problems, certainly, but the role of the church was seen to be crucial to the transfiguration of human life into divine life. Under strong dynasties of emperors, Constantinople more than ever felt itself to be the capital of the world — New Rome, head of civilization and bastion of the Christian faith. If the Byzantines came dangerously close to seeing the interests of Christ as identical with their own interests, so did the Latin church when it finally won the day in western Europe under a revitalized papacy. In placing pontifical authority above all temporal authority and powers, the papacy believed in its right to lead the world to a state of Christian order. The Byzantine East, however, believed that it already was that very Christian order. St. Augustine's warning of the dangers contained in confusing the City of God with the City of Man was lost on both sides. Such developments also did subtle damage to ecclesiology, to the understanding of the mystery of the church.

The result was that each society largely came to believe in its heart of hearts that it was the only legitimate and full form of Christianity which gave rise to a kind of 'we' and 'non-we' psychological outlook. The Latins most often behaved toward their Eastern brothers with clumsy boorishness and intransigence, while the Byzantines responded with haughty pride and calculation. Over these centuries, the ninth to the early thirteenth, missionary, economic and territorial rivalries, as well as deepening ignorance of each other's languages, temperaments and customs, further deepened the estrangement and fed the spirit of schism. This situation and atmosphere made it quite impossible for the churches to co-operate in solving the two issues of substance which needed to be addressed. These two issues were the question of the nature of the Pope's role in the church (other than his patriarchal role) and the question of the *filioque*, a phrase added to the Creed in the West concerning the procession of the Holy Spirit.[7]

Vladimir Lossky may indeed have been right when he said that the schism was 'a spiritual commitment, a conscious taking of sides in a matter of faith'[8] and thus the root cause of the East—West schism. The matter of faith he referred to, of course, was the matter of the *filioque* and the papal claims. Yet the historical context and the behaviors of the participants need to be considered to perhaps moderate his view, while detracting nothing from what may be essentially correct. That churchmen discussed

The Great Church of Holy Wisdom (Hagia Sophia), in Constantinople,
built by Emperor Justinian in the sixth century.

the Pope's claims and the Holy Spirit's procession in the same
breath as they caviled and disputed over whether priests should
be clean shaven, whether the lower clergy ought to be married or
celibate, whether the eucharistic bread should be leavened or
unleavened, or whether it was true that in the West women
frolicked with the priest during Mass, shows the unpropitious
human circumstances that prevailed for reaching any serious and
full discussion about what really matters.

Yet on two occasions, in the ninth and the eleventh centuries
when the churches were in actual schism, and as serious as these
occasions were, they seemed to heal themselves, at least to some
degree. There is ample evidence, even in the difficult years of the
early Crusade period, that communion in the sacraments continued, although not without incidents, between the faithful of
East and West.[9] The relationships of the churches were severely
strained at the level of the hierarchy and impaired at the level of
the people, but they had not been utterly destroyed. Some mutual
recognition of each other remained, if at times it seems vestigial.
Some rare souls with truly Christian insight recognized that the

situation was a disabling wound in the church. Peter of Antioch, after the rupture and scandal of 1054, exclaimed, 'If the queens of the earth (Old and New Rome) are at enmity, all the world will be in tears.' He is echoed by George the Hagiorite who pleaded in 1064 that 'There is no difference between Greeks and Latins.'[10]

The terrible events of the year 1204 when the armies of the Fourth Crusade were diverted to Constantinople instead of going to Palestine took the schismatic situation of the churches to the popular level and made the East–West schism absolute. After 1204 there can be no doubt whatsoever that the Christian East and West were utterly estranged. Who actually diverted the crusading host has not yet been settled by the historians, but there is no doubt whatever as to what actually happened during the three terrible days of 1204 when the Crusaders looted Constantinople.

'Even the Saracens are merciful and kind,' protested Nicetas Choniates, 'compared with these men who bear the Cross of Christ on their shoulders.' What shocked the Greeks more than anything was the wanton and systematic sacrilege of the Crusaders. How could men who had specially dedicated themselves to God's service treat the things of God in such a way? As the Byzantines watched the Crusaders tear to pieces the altar and icon screen in the Church of the Holy Wisdom, and set prostitutes on the Patriarch's throne, they must have felt that those who did such things were not Christians in the same sense as themselves.[11]

What did this catastrophe mean for western Europe and its development; indeed, what did it mean for mankind? Perhaps General Kireev's words best sum it up:

The greatest misfortune that befell mankind was, without doubt, the schism between Rome and the Ecumenical Church. The greatest blessing for which mankind can hope would be the reunion of east and west, the reconstitution of the great Christian unity.[12]

Each side, even while it claims to be Christ's one true church, must face the fact that humanly it has been profoundly impoverished by the separation. The Greek East and the Latin West needed and continue to need one another. For both of them the great schism has proved to be the greatest tragedy. Having lost communion with the East, Western Catholic Christianity developed a style of church which tended to be rather monolithic. The tendency to see the church as a society dependent on Divine Law, latent from earlier times, got rather out of control, a development which led to many of the Reformation's problems in the sixteenth century. The East, on the other hand, tended to split up into national churches and encountered enormous problems in practical unity and made concerted action when required almost impossibly difficult. The conditions of the modern world, the passing of time and the faithfulness of the Holy Spirit promise to bring the sister churches of Old and New Rome to new understanding and to draw upon each other's strengths and talents, a development which was quite impossible to contemplate in the centuries following the catastrophe of 1204 or in the poisonous ethos that produced it.

CHAPTER TWO

The Byzantine
Theological View

GOSPEL, CULTURE AND BYZANTIUM

Jesus Christ and his apostles preached only one gospel. This gospel is for all people and is addressed to all in their particular cultures. No particular culture, no matter how venerable or successful, can ever lay claim to being the only possible embodiment of Christ's gospel. Rather, the gospel can have as many embodiments as there are human communities in the world. The future may yet see other Catholic traditions appear. In African, Indian and Far Eastern cultures, this may already be happening. The process is not fixed in the past, but the past shows us something of its pattern.

From the earliest days the one gospel was expressed in multiple traditions. Basically, there are three of these: Latin, Middle Eastern and Oriental. Each has picked up the color of local societies and cultures, gathering together elements such as philosophical outlook, temperament and art and focusing them in the three great Catholic traditions. The subject of this study is the Orthodox group — those in the tradition of the Middle Eastern manifestation of the gospel, the Hellenistic (Greek) form of life in Christ.

The Middle Eastern tradition has some significant emphases in its externalization of the gospel. There are three that clearly arise from the first seven ecumenical councils,[13] all of which councils took place in the Hellenistic (Middle Eastern) church. The three marks, or emphases, were further reinforced by the great teachers of the faith in the Greek East, especially St. Gregory of Nyssa, St. Gregory Nazianzus, St. Basil and St. John Chrysostom. The three emphases, which derive from the councils and the fathers, are the Holy Trinity, the Incarnation and Repentance. Bearing in mind that belief is always expressed liturgically in Eastern Christianity, we shall examine these three characteristics.

The sacraments and worship of the East are always directed to the Triune God. Every service begins with a doxology (praise words: *doxa*, glory; *logos*, word). The invocation and praise of the Three Persons, One God, is repeated again and again in all the services. The same is true for the private prayer of the believer, which retains a liturgical form in the East.[14]

Among the Persons of the Holy Trinity, the Holy Spirit is liturgically prominent. He is described as God's 'Good, Holy and Life-Giving Spirit,' whose activity makes the Eucharist, sustains the church, and who is the source of all man's love, prayer and good works.[15]

The East's emphasis upon the Incarnation (God become man) derives from the councils of Ephesus (431) and Chalcedon (451).

These were the councils that battled for the ingredients of the Christ. The redeemer is true God and true Man, without confusion or alteration, in the one historical and ever-living person of Jesus Christ. The mystery of the Incarnation is the focal point to which everything is referred. Christ, the God—man, is the opening of the divine—human communion. This is the source of the church's nature and the ground of Christian life.

In the fullness of time, and by his own free will, the Word begotten of God the Father before all ages became incarnate of the woman who knew not carnal union. He suffered crucifixion and death, and by his resurrection He saved man who was dead from the beginning. (Stichera of Anatolios the Patriarch)

The liturgical prayers from these conciliar sources delight to dwell upon the wonder of the Incarnation. The Kanons (hymns) of the Octoechos (Eight Tones), which are the core of the repeating set of eight Sunday services, constantly present the theme to the heart of the believer.

O Christ, let us glorify your resurrection from the dead, by which you delivered the race of Adam from the slavery of Hades, and, being God, granted life everlasting and great mercy to the world.

The third characteristic mark, the theme of Repentance, is presented in the Eight Tones (Octoechos) of weekdays. The figures of the Harlot, the Publican in the Temple, and St. Peter struggling to believe, are gazed upon. The theme of Repentance is further distilled in the Great Kanon of Lent, as well as being externally and permanently manifest in monastic life.

Through heedlessness I have fallen into the heavy sleep of sin. But, my Christ, who for my sake hast fallen asleep on the Cross, do Thou awaken me, that the night of death comes not upon me. (Irmos of the Eighth Canticle of Matins, First Friday of Lent)

Repentance is not a thing of the moment. It is not an act for the death bed. The whole of life is Repentance, the struggle to realize and co-operate with the blessing of the Incarnation. Repentance is the ongoing entry to the life of the Resurrection. Although at every point it is clear that all strength, all blessing, all progress comes from God by the Holy Spirit, this does not mean that man is taken over. The East is not deterministic.

Carelessly I have wasted my life, and my soul is heavy with the drowsiness of sin. To thine unsleeping intercession, all pure Virgin, do I fly; let me not slumber in the sleep of death. (Theotokion, Matins, First Friday of Lent)

The Holy Trinity, a fifteeenth-century icon by St. Andrew Rublev. Described as a painter 'full of joy and brightness,' Rublev is a theologian of the mystery of the Trinity.

   Faith and culture in Eastern Christianity is a many-sided thing, arising from three distinct cultures. It is a fusion of Greek, Latin and Eastern elements, with contributions over time from the Slav peoples and other ethnic groups. From these cultures there arose a new and particular culture: a new rite, a church with a spirituality which was both universal and universalizing.[16] This is the

Byzantine church which takes its name from the town of Byzantium better known as Constantinople. At the heart of Byzantine Christianity are the three marks that we have explained: Trinity, Incarnation and Repentance. These distinguish the Byzantine approach to God, to Jesus Christ and to the nature of life in the world.

TRINITY AND INCARNATION

A Christian is not somebody who believes in God in general. A Christian is someone who believes that God is Father, Son and Holy Spirit.[17] This belief makes Christianity startlingly different among religions, even among the monotheistic religions, such as Judaism and Islam. To understand anything about the life of Eastern Christians one must constantly remember that life is grounded upon the mystery of the Holy Trinity. God is Father, Son and Holy Spirit. It is not an exaggeration to say that they see the life of the Christian as living in the loving embrace of the Holy Trinity.

The modern mind, with its strong tendency to rationalism (the impulse to explain and to dissect), most often sees the Trinity as a lofty doctrine, a mixture of theological abstraction and philosophical puzzle. The Christian East on the other hand sees the Trinity as the Ultimate Mystery, which, of course, has nothing to do with loftiness or abstraction. Since the mystery of the One God — Father, Son and Holy Spirit — is the source of all created reality, whether spiritual or earthly, the mystery of the Divine Trinity has everything to do with this world, humankind and myself. Therefore, any attempt to explain the world and man without reference to the Trinity is regarded as utterly futile, as unreal in the most fundamental sense.

The Eastern Christian understanding of God takes shape between two facts. God is radically unknowable, yet has made himself known. God is the unapproachable, yet he has approached mankind. To use theologians' words, God is the transcendent 'other,' yet he is the immanent 'thou.' How is this possible? Is it not a contradiction? With St. Gregory of Nyssa, Eastern Christianity says that 'to understand God, one has to be God' whose divine essence is 'incomprehensible.' Understanding that God's essence and being cannot be caught and defined in the frail net of human words, categories and mental strivings, Eastern Christianity also gives the strongest emphasis to God's self-revelation, a revelation that has taken place in its utter fullness in the mystery of the Incarnation, in the person of Jesus Christ. This emphasis is best seen in the writings of the great fathers of the East, and most notably in St. Gregory of Nyssa, St. Gregory Nazianzus, St. Maximus the Confessor and St. Gregory Palamas. These fathers pondered the 'taking of flesh' not because they wished to answer the philosophers' conundrum of how the Unknowable could become known, but precisely because the Unknowable *had* become known in Jesus Christ.

> At various times in the past and in various different ways, God spoke to our ancestors through the prophets; but in our own time, the last days, he has spoken to us through his Son ... the radiant light of God's glory and the perfect copy of his nature, sustaining the universe by his powerful command. (Hebrews 1:1–3)

It is simply not possible to appreciate Jesus Christ, comprehend his work of redemption or penetrate the Christian faith unless one is constantly alive to who Jesus Christ really is, Son of God, true God of true God. Jesus Christ is Yahweh, the God of Israel, who has broken into time and assumed human nature, who has become one with mankind. Without the Incarnation, Christianity would cease to have any meaning at all.[18] Because Jesus Christ is a true man and true God, Christians have a true communion with God. This relationship is not symbolic or external, legal or ethical. Nor is it merely moral. It is a living contact in 'the love of God made fully visible in Jesus Christ.' The fathers of the East (St. Gregory Palamas most lucidly of all) insist that through the God–man, Jesus Christ, man can directly know God. In the words of the Letter to the Hebrews:

> In other words, brothers, through the blood of Jesus we have the right to enter the sanctuary, by a new way which he has opened for us, a living opening through the curtain, that is to say, his body. (Hebrews 10:19–20)

With its theological view founded on the twin pillars of biblical realism and the creed of the great councils, the Eastern Christian church delights to dwell upon this mystery of mysteries. It constantly illuminates it in both the Holy Liturgy[19] and in the texts of the great feasts of the Christian year. The Hymn of the Incarnation from the Divine Liturgy prays:

> Only begotten Son and Word of God, immortal as you are, you condescended for our salvation to take flesh from the holy Mother of God and ever-virgin Mary, and without undergoing change, you became man. You were crucified, O Christ God, and crushed death by your death. You are One of the Holy Trinity, equal in glory with the Father and the Holy Spirit: save us!

The hymns from the feast of the Theophany[20] (the Baptism of Christ) sing of the mystery of the Incarnation and of the Trinity.

Gathering together biblical themes of both Testaments, as well as the teaching of the great councils on the Trinity and the Incarnation, the Eastern church has created the most exuberant and celebratory poetry ever formed in the church's tradition. Since barriers of language make access to these texts difficult, we will give a taste of them here at some length. These hymns are among the true treasures of the Byzantine church, the fruit of her living experience of the Christian mystery. No barbarian or infidel, physical calamity or godless oppression can ever rob her of them. While ever they are sung, the faith is taught.

The Troparion of the Feast shows that it is Jesus Christ who brings us to see God in a way never known by mankind. The revelation of the Holy Trinity occurs because of Jesus Christ.

> In the Jordan, when you were baptised, O Lord, the mystery of the Trinity was revealed, for the voice of the Father bore you witness by calling you 'Beloved Son,' and the Holy Spirit in the form of a Dove, confirmed the immutability of this declaration. O Christ God, who came forth and filled the world with light, glory to You!

This hymn is full of voices from the Scriptures. 'Let us make man in our own image, in the likeness of ourselves' (Genesis 1:26) takes on a meaning that is dumbfounding in its implications for mankind's destiny. God is recreating the world under the mastery of the New Adam, Jesus. The text of Genesis is lit up by the mystery of the person of Christ, the God–man. Human beings are not created merely to reflect God by being created with a mind and a will; rather, in Christ Jesus, the New Adam, man becomes God and God becomes man. The voice of St. Athanasius, in his great statement that 'God became man so that man might become God,' is heard to sound the concerted teaching of the church fathers on man's destiny, while the biblical foundations of their teaching are illuminated by the inspired voice of St. Peter: 'You will be able to share the divine nature' (2 Peter 1:4).

Through Jesus Christ man can be drawn into the heavenly sanctuary (Hebrews 10:19), the divine nature. With the Divine Son, who perfectly reflects the Father's glory, he will cry, in an ecstasy of love and awe, 'Abba! Father!' As in heaven, so on earth. The Christian prays this same prayer because being a Christian means to know that the time of metaphors has passed (John 16:25), that Jesus has achieved eternal life for man and that eternal life is to know the Father, the only true God and Jesus Christ, whom he has sent (John 17:3).

This is not a truth for the after-life. It is not something for the future. While Eastern Christianity insists that holiness is nothing less than participation in the life of the Trinity, it insists, just as

Icon of the Theophany or the Baptism of Christ. A Sicilian mosaic icon.

emphatically, that this participation begins in *this* world, in the dimension of time. The Eastern church does not see life as 'waiting' for God. With the apostle John, it sees *theosis*,[21] divinization, as beginning in time, in the 'now.' 'We [God, Father, Son and Spirit] shall come to him and make our home with him' (John 14:23).

The apostle Jude stands for all men upon whom the meaning of the teaching of Jesus is dawning, yet who hesitate to believe that something so amazing could be true. He asked Jesus, 'Lord, what is this all about? Do you intend to show yourself to us?' Jesus' answer, that he and the Father will 'make our home with him' and truly 'come to him,' fills the believer with joy and with a peace not known to the world. Yet it is so overwhelming a truth that it also fills the believer with reverence and awe. The first and second verses of the antiphons for the Lamplighting psalms, sung at the Vespers of the Theophany, touchingly and with great psychological insight, express this joyful awe when John the Baptist recognizes the Saviour's identity.

When the Forerunner saw Him who is our enlightenment, who enlightens everyman, coming to be baptised, his heart rejoiced while his hand trembled.

The Kontakion of the same feast makes it abundantly clear who Jesus Christ is for mankind.

> Today You have appeared to the world, O Lord, and your light has shone upon us who, realising who you are, sing to you a hymn of praise. Inaccessible light, You have come and made yourself known!

It is clear in this Kontakion that Jesus Christ is the light that shines in the dark (John 1:9), the one who in the beginning was with God, the Word who was God (John 1:1), the one who reconciles man with God (Colossians 1:20) yet who 'became as men are; and being as all men are, he was humbler yet, even to accepting death, death on a cross' (Philippians 2:7−8).

THE MYSTERY OF THE CHURCH

If asked to say what the church is, a post-Vatican II Catholic would answer in a flash to the effect that the church is the 'Body of Christ,' the 'People of God' or a 'Pilgrim People,' since for quite some time now in the West there has been a great deal of talk about the church in its most comprehensive sense. The same question put to a Byzantine Christian would not receive such a ready answer, and when it came it would take longer and need many more words. In its shortest form, the Byzantine answer would be that the church is 'a sacramental communion with God in Christ and the Spirit.'[22] Immediately we are returned to Trinity and Incarnation.

The Eastern Christian finds it easy enough to reply, but they do not really believe that too much talking about the church, beyond its basic fact, proves very much. The Orthodox believer, very much like the simple Catholic, knows that the church is 'the meeting place of all mysteries'[23] and so shows great reluctance to speak of the church, precisely because it is the mystery of the divine−human communion in time and space, a mystery which 'surpasses the capacities and powers of our intellect.'[24] They will almost never talk about the church 'from the outside,' as a 'thing' to be studied, as an 'object.' To the inexperienced, replies such as 'in our church we fast a lot,' 'in our church we have lots of icons,' 'in our church we baptize, chrismate (confirm) and give the Eucharist to our babies all at once,' may seem even a little beside the point, a little slow-witted. What they are really saying is, with Jesus, 'Come and see!'

There is almost an instinct which says that to speculate to no good purpose is dangerous. The instinct is a good one. It stops one from forgetting that we are the church ourselves; from be-

The Assembly of the Apostles, a seventeenth-century Greek icon.

coming a spectator at our own prayer, from turning theology into
mental geometry of the divine. For this reason, Christians of the
Byzantine churches describe themselves as 'Orthodox' in the Greek
language, or as 'Pravoslavnie' in the Slavonic tongue. To be an
Orthodox means to be 'right worshipping,' to be one who wor-

ships God as he desires to be worshipped, which is to say: in Spirit and in Truth through the Eucharist of his Son, Jesus Christ. Right belief is the guarantee of right worship.

The Eastern Christian sees the church as receiving self-understanding in being the church. The church reveals this identity when she teaches and celebrates the Holy Mysteries. Her being is revealed in her doing, in her *leiturgia*, to use the basic sense of the word. In short, the mystery of the church, as it is conceived by Eastern Christianity, is best approached in the church's worship, in what the church does. No celebration in the Byzantine calendar shows us this better than the Feast of Pentecost.

The Byzantine celebration of Pentecost is an exuberant feast. The aspects or themes interplay, one with another, to lead the worshipper into the mystery of God's outpouring of himself into the world, in the church. Pentecost is presented essentially as the dramatic and final revelation of God in time. God is filling all creation with his presence in the Holy Spirit, through the apostolic church.

Pentecost is also the final revelation of the truth of the Holy Trinity. Through the mystery of the Incarnation, God the Son, the 'Logos' who called everything into being from non-existence, came among us as a true man; so at Pentecost, the Holy Spirit, the same who inspired the prophets, parted the Red Sea and made Sinai flame and smoke, is revealed not as an impersonal force—idea, but as the person 'through whom we know the Father and glorify the Son' (Lamplighting Verses of Pentecost).

In the outpouring of the Holy Spirit the world, indeed the whole cosmos, becomes paradise restored, restored in the church. God first fills his church, the vessel of salvation, in founding it upon the charismatic persons of his apostles:

> The Holy Spirit provides every gift: He inspires prophecy, perfects the priesthood, grants wisdom to the illiterate, makes simple fishermen to become wise theologians, and establishes perfect order in the organisation of the Church. Wherefore, O Comforter, equal in nature and majesty with the Father and the Son, glory to you! (Stichera of Pentecost)

The holiness of the church is the holiness of the Holy Spirit. It is not man's holiness. It is God's gift. Infallibly, without fear of disappointment, the Christian believer receives the Spirit through the charismatic ministry of the apostles in the New Israel, the church.

> We have seen the true light, we have received the heavenly Spirit, we have found the true faith ... our Saviour through the prophets you have shown us the way to salvation, through the Apostles the grace of

your Holy Spirit has shone upon us. You are God from all eternity, our God, now and for endless ages. (Stichera of Pentecost, 5-7)

The outpouring of the Spirit throws creation into reverse, so to speak. Adam's sin altered the world. Man's very being, his fellows, nature and the whole universe once naturally bespoke of God, revealing the connectedness of all life in the creation. Sin opened man's eyes upon a world which had tragically altered. Man's self-understanding was now divided and partial. Filled with death, the works of man became futile vanities. He who was once made master of the cosmos became a victim. Reoriented upon the Divine Son, the world is recreated by the Spirit. It once more becomes paradise, the very threshold of heaven. Man, and because of him the cosmos, is recreated by the Spirit upon the New Adam, Jesus Christ, 'who emptied himself by leaving the bosom of the Father, assuming our human nature and making it divine' (Apolysis of Pentecost). What was shattered is restored, transfigured by divinity.

Through the church all creation is called once more to be a sacrament of God. As Ezekiel once foresaw, man is recalled to his natural unity, a unity, however, which does not obliterate personhood, since it is founded upon the Holy Trinity. All the demonic tyrannies, which with human collusion sought to dehumanize and depersonalize man, are revealed as counterfeits by the miracle of Pentecost. The barriers of sex, race, language and culture are dissolved in Pentecost's celebration of human variety. Man and woman are restored to each other as friends and lovers in the very spirit of the love of Jesus Christ for the church.

> In days of old, pride brought confusion of tongues to the builders of the Tower of Babel, but now the very diversity of tongues enlightened the minds and gave knowledge for the glory of God ... here there is variety so that voices could be joined in unison for the salvation of our souls. (Apostichon of Pentecost in the Eighth Tone)

The mystery of Pentecost reveals the catholicity of the church as a glorious liberation, of diversity in unity.

The Eastern church's approach to the faith Catholic is to be found in her art as well as in her poetry and hymns. The icon of Pentecost, like all icons, teaches the mystery in the midst of the liturgy. When the faithful enter the church on the eve of Pentecost Sunday and during Pentecost week, they first of all go to reverence the icon of the feast which is placed in the center of the church. They are reverencing the mystery which the icon makes present among them.

Represented in the icon are the Holy Spirit like tongues of fire, the Twelve Apostles and the curious figure of an old, old man at

Pentecost, from a Russian icon of the fifteenth century.

the very bottom of the icon. He stands for the cosmos, all that was deformed by Adam's sin, the world of man-alone, the created order, for all that is not God. Old Man Cosmos, his arms raised in supplication, begs to be received into their communion, which is to receive the divine gift of those anointed by the Holy Spirit.

*The earliest surviving icon of Pentecost. The Rabula Codex of 586. Mary,
Theotokos (God-bearer), in the mystery of the church and the world.
Overshadowed by the Holy Spirit at the Annunciation, Mary in her divine
Motherhood is made complete in her mothering of the church at Pentecost.*

(right)
*The Virgin Mother, Hodigritria, 'she who points the way' to the divine
Son. A unique rendering of the icon by Taikan Yokoyama. The lotus, the
flower of perfection and all spiritual sweetness, blooms in the foreground.*

He recognizes that the Holy Spirit is the gift that these men alone
infallibly bestow.

Some icons of Pentecost also portray Mary the Mother of God
as the central figure and standing in the midst of the apostles.
Like them she is overshadowed by tongues of fire. Who is Mary?
She is the Mother of the Holy Church, the New Eve, 'the mother

of all those who live' (Genesis 3:20). From the womb of Eve came all mankind, but from her rebellious conspiracy with Adam came sin and death. The obedience of the New Eve, Mary, overshadowed by the Spirit, made possible the Saviour's incarnation for man's salvation and life.

> ... for your praise is beyond the eloquence of the most cultured tongues. The wonderful manner in which you gave birth to Christ throws every intelligence into amazement. Therefore the faithful magnify you with one accord. (Hirmos of Pentecost)

Like Catholics, Orthodox Christians cannot see how Christianity can be anything but diminished by neglect of the Theotokos[25] (she who gave birth to God). Jesus is not glorified if she is denigrated.

Grouped around the New Eve, the church, for whom Christ the New Adam is the cornerstone, the apostles are her foundation.[26] The apostles are those by whose authority and ministry the church is directed on its way to the kingdom of God.[27] It is the apostles who declare that something 'seems good to the Holy Spirit and to us.' The apostolic authority in the service of the kingdom has devolved upon their successors, the bishops of the church. The power of the bishop is the power of the apostles, a power of grace that sacrifices to God, heals and sanctifies human activities and gives them glory by absorbing them into the kingdom of God.[28] In the East there exists no higher power than that of a bishop. As St. Cyprian declared, 'You must realize that a bishop is constituted by his church and a church by her bishop; whoever is not with his bishop is not in the church.' This means that every church united to its bishop is the catholic and apostolic church of Jesus Christ in its fullness.

THE BISHOP IN THE CHURCH

Orthodoxy does not see the gospel as a disembodied ideology. A Christian is not someone who comes to the teachings of Jesus Christ as to a more or less private and individual experience. Conversion to Jesus is not solitary. Rather, at the very instant that the Holy Spirit bestows the divine grace of adoption, a man ceases to be alone. He enters God's *oikos*, God's house and family. Likewise, the apostles are not teachers of a mere body of knowledge. They are witnesses to Jesus Christ in whom mankind is drawn to the Father in the Holy Spirit. The apostles do not make individual converts who can bury their one talent in some privatized Christian life; rather, they initiate men and women

'The mercy of Our Lord Jesus Christ and God the Father and the community of the Holy Spirit be with you all.'

into the life of Christ's body, the church. Wherever the apostle or bishop is found, the wonder of the Incarnation is manifested in the Eucharist and the life of the Trinity is revealed in community. Consequently, the role of the bishop is of first importance for understanding in what spirit the Eastern churches are organized and for feeling something of the inner atmosphere of the communities of the church. The ministry of the apostle is permanently maintained in the church by the bishop.

As God the Father is the principle of unity in the Holy Trinity, the bishop is endowed by the Holy Spirit to maintain and manifest the unity of the church. As God the Father presides in the love-union of the Holy Trinity, eternally begetting the Son and breathing forth the Spirit, the bishop brings among men the mystery of Jesus in the Eucharist, bestowing and sharing the Spirit among the believers. In the early church the bishop was the only celebrant of the Eucharist.

I exhort you to strive to do everything in a divine harmony under the leadership of the bishop who holds the place of God the Father. (St. Ignatius of Antioch)

In the liturgy of Byzantium, the bishop moves, acts and prays as the one who manifests the presence of the Holy Trinity in the church.

The bishop is vested with the *sakkos* (outer garment) symbolizing the divine splendor of Jesus. Around his shoulders he wears the *omophorion*[29] (great stole) which signifies the Incarnation 'by which Christ took upon himself our human nature and restored it to the Father.' The bishop dresses in the middle of the church before every liturgy he celebrates, as a powerful example of the liturgy teaching the mysteries. As the *omophorion* is placed on his shoulders the deacon proclaims: 'On your shoulders, O Christ, you placed our wayward nature; in your Ascension you presented it to the Father.' Crowned with the miter, symbol of the Father's majesty and power, the bishop blesses all those assembled. Many times throughout the liturgy he bestows the blessing. When he does so he holds two sets of candles in his hands. In his right hand, the *trikerion*, a triple candle representing the Holy Trinity; in his left hand, the *dikerion*, a double candle symbolizing the God–man Jesus Christ in his divine and human natures. Yet the bishop is a man like any other. The liturgy reminds one of this when the Book of Gospels is carried through the church in procession at the Little Entrance. At the Gospel's approach, the bishop stands at the sanctuary gates. He puts aside the miter, the great stole, his staff of pastoral authority, as the very word of the heavenly Master, Jesus Christ, is proclaimed. Like any other Christian the bishop must listen humbly to the word of the Master in the Holy Scriptures. Before the presence of Christ in the Gospels he stands bare-headed and attentive.

The symbolism of the liturgy is rich and complex, representing the many-sided mystery of God's saving work among men. The Orthodox liturgy clearly shows that the rights and powers of the bishop belong to another order. They cannot be compared to worldly power structures, since they are for the service of the church's communion, a communion which must be lived in love and freedom. Since the bishop bestows the Spirit, the very Spirit who sets man free and makes him a son, the bishop's rights and powers go to create that very freedom. Without the proper exercise of the bishop's ministry, true freedom in the Spirit is endangered. Without its bishop, the church would degenerate either into an abstract ideal or into an individual spiritual life in an invisible church. The office of the bishop, which is that of the apostle, is fundamental in the Byzantine understanding of the church, as it is in the Western Catholic tradition. Like the apostles of old, the bishop is the servant of the mystery of 'the infinite treasure of Christ,' the one who shows clearly to all 'how the mystery is to be dispensed' (Ephesians 3:8–9).

The Byzantine view, like the Catholic, stresses that the church is a reality that transcends immediate expression. It is fellowship with God and man, the living opening to divine life (Hebrews 10:19−20). The East has a particularly vivid sense of the mystery of the church, a mystery in which all the baptized with their bishop are participants, which creates a strong communal feeling in the inner atmosphere of the Orthodox churches. This communal sense has been the foundation of the Eastern church's wider mission. The inner atmosphere of the Western Catholic church is complementary to that of the Byzantine. Beginning from the same understanding of divine−human fellowship, the Western emphasis falls upon the church as a divine society, an emphasis which gives rise to the West's strong concern for the world and for man.

With only a too thin knowledge of the Eastern church's splendid liturgy as an indicator, Catholics are likely to be misled into thinking that the Byzantine church must be a very clerical church. The opposite is the case, but this is not to say that the East in any way devalues the hierarchy or the hierarchical principle in Christianity. The hierarchy of bishop, priest and deacon is seen as a gift of the church. The power of the bishop to bind and loose is a power at the service of the believer and the community, not a power set over it. If this were not the case, hierarchy would be the very enemy of Christian freedom. Rather, hierarchy is something willed by Jesus Christ for the church. The prayer of consecration for the ordination of a bishop reveals the evangelical sources of the apostolic hierarchy.

> O Lord our God, who, forasmuch as it is impossible for the nature of man to endure the Essence of the Godhead, in thy providence has instituted for us teachers of like nature with ourselves, to maintain thine Altar, that they may offer unto thee sacrifice and oblation for all thy people; do then, the same Lord, make this man also, who hath been proclaimed a steward of the episcopal grace, to be an imitator of thee, the true Shepherd who didst lay down thy life for the sheep; to be a leader of the blind, a light to those who are in darkness, a reprover of the unwise, a teacher of the young, a lamp to the world; that, having perfected the souls entrusted to him in this present life, he may stand unashamed before thy throne, and receive the great reward which thou hast prepared for those who have contended valiantly for the preaching of the Gospel.

The bishop is not a monarch in the worldly sense, nor is hierarchy authoritarian. He is the image of God the Father, whom St. Ignatius described as 'the bishop of all.' The bishop is a monarch whose one power or rule is to guarantee the church's unity. Once more we are returned to contemplate the Holy Trinity.

A moment in the liturgy of Christmas in the Russian church.

A bishop without a community is a nonsense. A community without a bishop is equally absurd, as is a God who is not Trinity, or a God who is multiple. The Trinity is not the Father alone. Without the Son and the Spirit, God would become a remote and infinitely distant monad. He would dissolve into deep spaces beyond the created world and mankind. There would be no possible communion with him. Likewise, without the Father, God would dissolve into the created world, becoming Mother Nature, the Spirit of the World, or something equally pagan. The revelation of God as Trinity, Father, Son and Holy Spirit means

The Holy Cross by which the waters are blessed at the Feast of the Theophany (Baptism of Christ).

that communion with God is possible for man. The bishop and the community of believers reflect the mystery of the Trinity, the revelation of God's intimate reality. The church, then, is not its bishop. The church is not the *laos*, the people, but the church is seen wherever the Eucharist is offered; wherever the community is gathered around its bishop in the celebration of the eucharistic sacrifice. Consequently, any person or group that falls away from the church is said to have lost or to have broken communion. The bishop also has the special responsibility of maintaining unity and fellowship with the other churches, of defending the faith against heresy and of participating in ecumenical synods and episcopal councils.

Understanding that the church was entrusted to and founded upon the apostles, the best Orthodox theologians do not derogate Peter's place in the church, if he presides there in love. As the Father, the Son and the Holy Spirit are co-equal, so are those who bear their likeness in the world, in time and in human society. Consequently Orthodox theologians can see a special place for the Bishop of Rome among his brothers. Indeed, the Orthodox church has always been prepared to acknowledge this special place, this primacy, if the churches return to union. The Orthodox could see the Pope as one who is given to the church to serve the church's unity; to promote fellowship among the bishops, and hence among the churches, and to manifest the universal church. Like the Catholics, the Orthodox see primacy as an indispensible characteristic of the church and as a service to the church. Primacy promotes effective fellowship between particular churches and deepens and protects their organic bond. It works against broad and hollow indifference passing itself off as unity. Primacy in the church stands in the way of any tendency to reduce the universal church to a mere logical concept, which is to say from any approach to church which, while regarding the parts of the church as real, goes on to see the whole church as a subjective abstraction. The Orthodox already agree that the one who would be first in the church when its schism is healed is the Bishop of Rome, the Pope. As in earlier days, they would see him exercising a special concern to call to the churches in times of special danger and emergency, but they do not see the office of Peter as something to do with universal rule. They would agree with Patriarch Maximos IV of Antioch who observed that the 'You are Peter' of St. Matthew should never be separated from the 'Lend strength to your brothers' of St. Luke.

Most of the parish clergy of the Eastern church are married; the bishop, however, is always a monk. He is a monk in order that he might be entirely free to minister to his church, to his clergy and people, and in order that he might constantly ponder the word of truth and so teach his people authentically of Christ. The bishop is also a monk so that he may be a true father to his priests and people, sensitive to their needs and problems. His monastic vows are a sign that he will also 'lay down his life' for them (John 10:11, 15). This is not to say that 'episcopal absolutism' or 'despotism' is utterly unknown in the East.[30] Indeed, there is a sense in which such a tendency to 'Lord it over them like the pagans' is almost inevitable in the life of the church, inasmuch that Jesus specifically warned his apostles against its appearance. On the whole, the Eastern church has been less inclined to cast the bishop into a quasi-princely role, as perhaps the West once did.

HOLY TRADITION

Tradition is a word that has gone a little sour in the modern world. It seems to evoke associations from a dead past, all that is backward looking, something that is rigid and impersonal. Tradition, in the Christian East, certainly has a backward gaze to the past, but it is understood as a living thing. While tradition has specific contents drawn from the past, it is not an authority to whom one resorts when a point is to be proved. It is not merely a churchy form of archeology. Tradition could be better thought of as the ferment of the Holy Spirit going on in the heart of the church. In that sense, Tradition *is* the church. It is 'the continuity of divine assistance, the abiding of the Holy Spirit,'[31] which began with Pentecost and which has never ended. To be a member of the church, whether bishop, monk, layman or priest, is to be immersed in Tradition and to be responsible for it as a bishop, and responsive to it as one of the baptized. The rule of faith in the Eastern church is Tradition, the measure of Christian reality both doctrinally and sacramentally.

The church and sacred Tradition enjoy a unity like to body and spirit. They cannot be separated without the death of both elements. The church possesses Tradition as the body possesses its own living principle. Naturally sacred Tradition has elements which go to make it up.

> Some things we have from written teaching, others we have received from the Apostolic Tradition handed down to us in a mystery; and both these things have the same force of piety. (St. Basil)

The Eastern church places the Scriptures themselves, the seven ecumenical councils, the creeds of the universal church, the teaching of the church fathers, the canons of church law and customs, the church's worship and its art within Tradition. All of these elements, including the Holy Scriptures, are the works of the church in the Holy Spirit. Although it is the most profound thing, holy Tradition is finally very simple. It is nothing less than the preaching of 'the new life that came forth from the empty tomb.'[32] Everything in the church's life which makes this new life manifest and which gives men and women access to the Risen Christ, no matter how humble, belongs within holy Tradition.

It should be no surprise for Catholics to learn that the Orthodox place the Holy Scriptures within Tradition. The Orthodox have never had a chicken-and-egg problem with the relationship of Scripture and Tradition. The living experience of Jesus Christ comes first. Not merely as a record of it, but in response to it, the apostles and evangelists wrote God's sacred word in the Holy Spirit who had been poured out upon the church. In other words, the Scriptures did not write the church. Rather in the persons of her inspired apostles and evangelists, the church wrote the Scriptures. Only in the apostolic church is it possible to interpret the Holy Scriptures with authority. Like Catholics, Orthodox people accept the guidance of the church when they read the Scriptures. This is made very clear when a convert is received. They promise that 'I will accept and understand Holy Scripture in accordance with the interpretation which was held and is held by the Holy Orthodox Catholic Church of the East, our Mother.' Like Catholics, Orthodox people do not see this as authoritarian or in any way opposed to the freedom of the believer. They know only too well that it is only within the church's tradition that the believer will be free to hear the theme of the Holy Spirit in the Scriptures. Even the Holy Scriptures can be torn apart in a Babel of private interpretation (a parody of Pentecost) if they are taken out of the living Tradition.

The Scriptures are sacramental in Orthodox thinking, in that they make the mystery of Jesus present to the believer. Regarding the Bible as a verbal icon (image) of Christ, the Seventh Ecumenical Council decreed that the holy icons and the Book of the Gospels should be venerated in the same way. In every church the Gospel book has a place of honor on the altar; it is carried in procession at the Liturgy and at Matins on Sundays and Feasts; the faithful kiss it and prostrate themselves before it. It is particularly the constant study of the bishop, but also of his ministers, who preach in his churches, whether priests, monks or laymen.

Holy Tradition is as wide and as deep as the church itself. No aspect of authentic and time-honored Christian life lies outside of its embrace. The prayer forms of the devout believer, the design of the church services, the art, music and drama of the church's liturgy, the great truths defined by the ecumenical councils, the family, the priesthood and the service of the poor or the witness of the monks, all belong within Tradition. Certainly there is a hierarchy in the elements that go to make up sacred Tradition, but the unity of holy Tradition, as deep and as comprehensive as the church, embraces every element, despising none for its littleness.

THE *LAOS*, PEOPLE OF GOD

To be a layman is much more than not being a priest. A man or woman becomes *laikos*, a layman, or a full member of the *laos*, the people of God, by the gift of the Holy Spirit in chrismation. It follows that priests and deacons also belong to the *laos*. There is a sense in which laity includes clergy, but as the apostle in the church, the bishop is the one person who is not lay. This matter needs to be recast in other language. All of the baptized belong to the people of God. The baptized are the people of God, the body of Christ, and include all of those who will become bishops or clergy. The bishop and his clergy are part of the people of God, but have a special ministerial responsibility for the church, for their brothers and sisters. Because he has been received into the body of the apostles, the bishop calls the *laos* to himself. He constitutes it. That is, he makes the *laos* possible. In the same way that all things proceed from God and return to God, in the diocese all the blessings of Christ proceed from the bishop and are gathered together in the faithful assembled with him for the Eucharist. When bishop, priest, deacon and people gather, the whole priesthood of Christ is present in its diverse forms, for all of which the bishop is the source. This respects God's own mystery in the church 'for everything in him is a proceeding from one principle, a communication to several, and a perfect communion in unity.' God's own mystery, of course, is the Blessed Trinity.

The ministerial priesthood represents Christ sacramentally, while it also conforms to the relationship of the Christ to his church. Jesus is the head of his body, the church, and as such, he is one with his church, within the church. He is not above it or separate from it, yet he constitutes it. He is its cornerstone, the one High Priest (archihiereus) of the people of God. All share in his priesthood in the sacraments of Baptism and Chrismation, yet each of the baptized fulfills their part according to the gifts given to them, by their state and function in the church. All the believers share in the royal and priestly dignity of the whole body of Christ and all are called to be active in building up the people of God, yet not all are equal or the same. The Orthodox East is committed to the hierarchical principle in the church, as is the West, since it is a reflection of the very mystery of Christ in time. Indeed, it is its guarantee. However, like the Catholic West, the Orthodox, following the great fathers, also insist that the believers, the *laos*, are also necessary, not merely that the church might exist as an institution, but that the church may fulfill its divine mission and realize itself fully as the body of Christ. The East very clearly sees that by God's design the church does not exist for itself, so to speak. As Christ died for the world, the church exists for the world. The Byzantine liturgy constantly prays for this 'union of all.' Thus, it is the lay person, most especially, whose role it is to 'bring together under Christ all the wealth of creation and the virtualities that mankind can achieve.'

The Eastern church's practice supports its official theology. From very early days laymen have been involved in theology. Photius, Patriarch of Constantinople, famous for his rebuking of the West in the matter of the *filioque* (see page 21) was a layman and theologian before he became Patriarch. Laymen as theologians continue today in all the Orthodox churches. Many Orthodox bishops have lay theologians among their permanent advisers. Most of the education of the clergy, particularly in Greece, is in the hands of lay professors of theology. Most of the students and graduates of the theological faculties of Greece are laymen, the majority of whom remain so all their lives. The graduates with theological degrees do much of the preaching in the village churches of Greece, handle almost all of the catechetical instruction of the young, and are those responsible for the running of the many youth and home missions that sprang up in Greece earlier this century. This pattern holds for most other Orthodox countries.

At almost all levels of church life, the laity are actively involved. The College of the Bishops is *the* teacher of the faith to the whole church, while the people of God are the witness of Tradition. Even in ecumenical councils the people have a part to play, though not as if a democracy. Eastern Christians would never dispute that a council's deliberations and the responsibility for its decisions lie with the bishops. But the bishops would not dispute their responsibility to consult the laity in the discussions and debates, short of the final decision and promulgation of the decrees of the episcopate. Episcopal collegiality has been operative in the East and it recognizes that collegiality has a context. It is not *other* to the church. However, the laity do not assent to a council's decisions in the manner of an electorate. The bishop is the teacher of the faith, the laity its witness. The laity express themselves by 'living' the council.

In the new lands, as well as in the home countries of eastern Europe, the role of the laity is still clear and extensive. The communal principle of the church is strong in the East. Lay parishioners play a much more prominent role in all of the financial, social and decision-making arrangements for their churches and communities than do their Catholic counterparts. The bishop appoints the parish clergy, but the parish exercises extensive control over the use of the church and its resources. A parish priest who ignored his people's legitimate and true wishes would be very foolhardy.

The Orthodox do not look upon a layman as peculiar if he takes an interest in theology. As we have noted, it has never been a clerical preserve. His interest might make him a serious man but because there is no great lay–clerical antagonism, he is most often preserved from becoming merely bumptious or church obsessed. We should say one more thing about the East's attitude to theology. From the times of the great fathers, the East has been very wary of what a Catholic might call academic theology. The fathers always regarded theology (*theologia*) as 'the experiential way of union with God,' which is to say that, properly understood, theology is prayer. In this view, every Christian who is in the way of union with God is a true theologian. The Holy Spirit made them so when he sealed them in chrismation. When the Christian prays, when he witnesses to the faith in his confirmed role as prophet, he is a theologian. Theology, therefore, is not mere knowledge.

It should be obvious that the layman is no mere cipher in the Byzantine tradition. A layman can be a theologian, an adviser to bishops, a person responsible for the material needs of the church, one actively involved in the church's philanthropy, responsible for building up the community life of the church, and particularly if a married person, one responsible for nurturing the domestic church, the family. Above all, the lay people are witnesses to holy Tradition, in that they witness to it by living it, by applying it to their life lived in the world. This is their essential witness.

In the interest of presenting a realistic picture of Orthodox thinking about the laity, one is obliged to note a development among some Orthodox thinkers in the last one hundred and fifty years or so. The new development can be summed up best in a statement of Khomiakov, a Russian writer, who claimed that

The unvarying constancy and the unerring truth of Christian dogma does not depend upon any hierarchical order; it is guarded by the totality, by the whole people of the Church, which is the Body of Christ.[33]

This development is rather worrying from the Catholic point of view, as it is to more serious Orthodox theologians, since both the spirit and the content of this new teaching are eccentric. It is not truly Orthodox.

Driven by a very anti-Catholic animus, Khomiakov desired to distance Orthodoxy as far as it was possible from the Catholicism he so loathed and misunderstood. Unable to abide its strong emphasis upon the hierarchical principle in the church he turned to rather Protestant ideas and intruded them into his ecclesiology, such that his final position is quite contrary to the faith of the seven ecumenical councils acknowledged by the Orthodox church. In no place do they stress the people's guidance, nor do they teach that Tradition is guarded by the *laos*. While it is true that once the people of God accept ecumenical truth they keep it longer than any individual bishop is able to do, it is simply untrue to say that the Eastern church disputes guidance from above. To say such a thing is against the whole pattern of the Incarnation. In the same way that the divine nature of Jesus is the ordering principle in the person of Jesus, the hierarchical function assures the church's structure as the means of salvation and is essential to the church's existence.

Khomiakov's view is also curiously a-historical. It ignores the fact that the real actors in the great councils were patriarchs, popes, bishops and emperors. It was not the people who settled the question of Easter celebration, the baptism of heretics or the veneration of icons.

Taken literally, Khomiakov's view would cause the whole of Orthodox ecclesiology to dissolve. It would destroy any right understanding of the very body of Christ, since it would detach understanding the church from the person of Jesus Christ and from the mystery of the Incarnation. In the place of the body of Christ there would be a kind of amorphous populism. Khomiakov's idea of the people as guardian of the faith has more in common with Karl Marx's claims for the proletariat than it has with Eastern Orthodoxy's tradition. Clearly, one must keep one's eyes upon Christ when thinking about the church. To be motivated by anything other than Christ, as he is understood in ecumenical[34] tradition, will necessarily produce distortions.

The stress in the Western Catholic church has tended to fall upon the hierarchical principle. In the East it is upon the communal principle. However, each acknowledges the other. These are not contradictory, in the same way that the divine and human in Jesus are not contradictory. The East, however, tends to put more stress on *how* all share that in which the hierarchical principle resides. To use more immediate terms: the East emphasizes *how* the baptized share in the life and person of Jesus, the person of Jesus being constituted primarily by the fact that he is 'God from true God.' East and West express variously the two fundamental and complementary aspects of the church: the hierarchical and the communal principle. It is only when one understands the two together that one glimpses the fullness of the church, as well as the depth of the scandal of schism that still prevails.

'Preserve him in your holiness, strengthen him in the true faith, deliver him from the evil one, so that he may become a son and inheritor of your heavenly kingdom.'

CHAPTER THREE

The Sacramental Mysteries

AN APPROACH TO THE SACRAMENTS

Eastern Christians are sacramental realists and probably a great deal more surefooted in their approach to the sacraments than many in the contemporary West. They can perhaps be a strength to the West in a difficult time in which some Christians advocate a kind of high spiritualist approach to the sacraments against others who seem distinctly secularist. Whether it is the tendency to see the sacraments as spiritual channels in some divine hydraulics of grace, or as merely human festivals of religious allegory, both of these tendencies are unwelcome in the East, although they are not unknown there. The sacraments are neither aids to the spiritual life nor mere adornments to it. The sacraments *are* the spiritual life. They are life in Christ. St. John Chrysostom makes this abundantly clear when he writes of the Eucharist: 'We become one holy ... members of his flesh, bone of his bones. That is what the food that he gives us effects.'[35]

Catholics would be surprised to learn that Protestants seem very Catholic indeed in Orthodox eyes. The controversies over justification by faith and good works lead the East to suspect that the ghost of Pelagius has never really been laid in the West.[36] Whenever the sacraments are presented as merely 'fueling' Christian action in the world, good works are given implicit autonomy. The East insists that the life in Christ is one reality. Sacramental life *is* life in Christ, consequently care of the poor and all good works proceed from the Eucharist. It was in the very midst of the first Eucharist that Jesus washed the feet of his apostles. Service is an integral part of Eucharist. One flows into the other. The flow has one direction. It should not be reversed.

As noted elsewhere, the East sees Christian reality as life in Christ, not as imitation of Christ: to be Christ, not to be like Christ. Mere imitation runs the risk of reviving Pelagius' idea that Jesus, as a kind of superstar, or as 'the most perfect human being that existed,' was given to man as the supreme good example for man to follow. This implies that man is a self-saving being who really only needs inspiration, rather than salvation. In the same way that this view impairs the proper view of sacramental life, the church itself deteriorates from being the communion of saints in the life-creating sacraments, to become an association of self-saving saints. Such an association has no need of sacraments. The only organizing principle it needs is a constitution of some sort, which is to say, law, or failing that, a shared enthusiasm. The Christian East finds all of these tendencies terrible to contemplate. The rigidity of law is their least favorite. To the East, law can be the very death blow to life in Christ and to the world.

The East celebrates the same seven sacraments as the Catholic

PHOTOGRAPH BY K. HARKINS

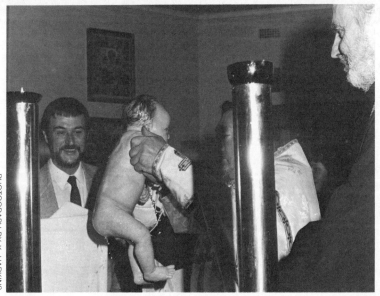

Baptism, the second birth and the gracious renewal of the entire being.

West. The seven sacraments communicate one reality: the reality of a living communion with God in Jesus Christ through the Holy Spirit. The sacraments are never separated from one's spiritual life. In the same way, the East does not see any split between the monastic cell and the church. Rather, prayer appropriates sacramental reality, while the reality of the sacraments provokes prayer. Taking the words of Jesus to the Samaritan woman quite literally, the church applies them to the sacraments as to life in Christ.

> Believe me, woman, the hour is coming when you will worship the Father neither on this mountain nor in Jerusalem. You worship what you do not know; we worship what we do know ... But the hour will come — in fact it is here already — when worshippers will worship the Father in spirit and truth. (John 4:21−23)

Both prayer and the sacraments in the Byzantine view place the believer in a direct communion with the Father through the mystery of the Incarnation.

Byzantine theology, like Catholic theology, sees the sacraments as having a cosmic significance. The world is being recreated by the Holy Spirit in the sacraments. They achieve creation's return to God. They show the connectedness of life. They return man's being to its true nature in *theosis*, to becoming God, in the prayer of sacramental worship.

EUCHARIST

The Divine Liturgy (the Mass) holds the very first place in the worship of the East, as it does in the Catholic West. It is *the* action in which the Church most clearly reveals its nature; as the mystery of God in time, the body of Christ. In the sacred action of the Divine Liturgy Jesus Christ is revealed and made present among mankind. Word and song, color and movement, and the gifts themselves, point to the wonder of the Incarnation come into the present. The present (and all time) is caught up in the 'now' of the Incarnation. The stuff of the world and mankind becomes Jesus Christ in the bread and wine of the Eucharist. This wonder is brought about, not by man, but by the Holy Spirit.

> Moreover, we offer you this spiritual and bloodless sacrifice, and we pray and beseech You: send down Your Holy spirit upon us and upon these gifts lying before us, and make this bread the precious Body of Your Christ. Amen.
> And that which is in this cup the precious Blood of Your Christ. Amen.
> Having changed them by Your Holy Spirit. Amen. Amen. Amen.
> (Epiclesis of the Byzantine Liturgy)

There is no question that the East's belief in the true presence of Christ in the Eucharist is not identical to the faith of the Catholic West. The East, however, has a much less forensic approach. It almost never talks about 'matter' and 'form,' 'substance' and 'accidents,' and it uses the word 'transubstantiation' only very reluctantly — usually only in dialogue with the West. Beyond saying that the wonder of the Eucharist comes about by the power of the Holy Spirit, it is not really interested in knowing the 'how' of the real Presence. The Holy Spirit *is* the 'how' of the Eucharist. But the East is as deeply attached to the 'what' of the Eucharist as is the Roman church. While a Catholic would say that Jesus is present 'Body, blood, soul and divinity,' the Eastern Christian would say that he is present 'through and through' under the appearance of bread and wine. It is to say the same thing.

Only the baptized celebrate the Eucharist, but they do so not merely for themselves. Holding up the consecrated gifts, the priest prays:

> Remembering, therefore, this solitary precept and all that was done on our behalf: the cross, the tomb, the resurrection on the third day, the ascent into heaven, the sitting at the right hand of the Father, the second and glorious coming, we offer You Your own from what is Yours, in all and for all. (Prayer at the Elevation)

Rejoicing in having found Christ and being fed on him, the Christian prays that all mankind, all life, might find its way to the Author of Life, Jesus Christ, in the Eucharist. The most favored title for God, used over and over again in the East's liturgy is *philanthropos*, Lover of Man.

Following the great images explored by the church fathers, the East conceives of the Eucharist as at the very heart of the church. Jesus Christ is the very Tree of Life who confers immortality and divine sonship in the midst of the new paradise. This is the fellowship of the Holy Spirit, the church. In the sacred action of the liturgy (*leiturgia*), the baptized have access to the tree of abundant life, while the very fact of the celebration is both an invitation and a drawing to the mystery of all those who seek God of sincere heart, the secret Christians, as yet unbaptized. So that the Eucharist may be for all men in all times, it is found in the somewhere and in the sometime of the church.

The reverence of Eastern Christians toward the sacraments is much deeper than their Catholic counterparts, at least externally. Before approaching the Holy Eucharist an Orthodox layman will fast for three days, go to confession and eat and drink nothing from the midnight before Communion. As he approaches the priest to receive the sacred elements it is not unusual for him to ask forgiveness of people he passes in the church, and to be congratulated on his return home by his friends and his family. Reception of the Eucharist is also much more infrequent: Easter, Christmas, Our Lady's Assumption and one's own feast day. The modern Catholic attitude of frequent Communion seems rather casual to the Orthodox. Children are the exception in the East. Children are admitted to Communion and are encouraged to go very often. Of course there have been various movements in the East to encourage older Christians to receive Communion more frequently, but things change slowly in Eastern sacramental practice.

Every Orthodox and Eastern Catholic church reserves the blessed sacrament in the church, but there are no eucharistic devotions outside of the liturgy. There is no equivalent of anything like Benediction of the Blessed Sacrament. The only time that the people are blessed with the sacrament occurs immediately after Holy Communion, and within the liturgy itself. This occurs just before the priest takes the remaining sacred elements to the table of preparation where they are consumed and the sacred vessels washed. Communion is always under both kinds and the bread used is leavened bread, baked as a small loaf. Communion is given from the chalice. The consecrated bread is given to the communicant soaked in the consecrated wine, using a special spoon.

Catholics can go to Holy Communion in a Catholic church of Eastern rite at any time, such as in the Catholic Ukrainian church, the Melkite church or the Catholic Russian church, but they should never attempt to do so in an Orthodox church. Even if a Catholic has come to love the Orthodox and the East, it is better to bear the personal pain of separation than to give offense or cause embarrassment. Finally, there is a point in Catholic canon law of which almost all Catholics are ignorant. If for a good reason (including education) Catholics attend the Holy Liturgy in an Orthodox church on a Sunday, they have fulfilled their Sunday obligation. They do not have to go to Mass again in a Catholic church.

MARRIAGE

The kingdom of God is not something beyond this life or found only at its end. The kingdom is present in our midst whenever the will of God is 'done on earth, as it is in heaven.' While the fullness of the kingdom is revealed face to face beyond death, it is also a this-world experience. The Christian life in Christ, in the sacramental communion of the church, 'is like the yeast a woman took and mixed in with three measures of flour till it was leavened all through' (Matthew 13:33). It is a mystery, a great mystery, one concerning 'Christ and the Church' (Ephesians 5:32). The church is the macrocosm of this mystery of divine–human communion. The sacrament of Marriage is the microcosm of this mystery, the domestic church. Beginning as natural marriage, the love of man and woman becomes a sacrament in the church, for the world.

The wedding service in the Eastern tradition consists of two parts. The first part, or the betrothal (in some churches celebrated separately), is followed by the crowning, the preferred term for the marriage service. The betrothal brings human love to the threshold of the kingdom and it takes place at the door of the church, or just inside. The couple are natural man who thirst for fulfillment and redemption. 'O Lord our God,' says the priest, 'who has espoused the Church as a pure Virgin from among the Gentiles, bless this betrothal, and unite and maintain these Thy servants in oneness of mind' (Byzantine Betrothal Service). This oneness of mind was shattered in the mutual recriminations and hostilities of the first parents (Genesis 3:12–13). The betrothal service stands as the 'vestibule of the kingdom: both beginning and exile.'[37]

The couple are then led in procession into the church. That which was fallen enters into the kingdom. 'Eros,' humanly noble,

*The crowning of man and woman signifies the dignity and purity of
marriage. Each is each other's crown.*

becomes 'agape,' the love of the saints. In this procession the
world enters the 'world to come.' The couple are then crowned
(with metal crowns in Russia, or with crowns of flowers in Cyprus
or Greece) while the priest prays, 'O Lord and God, crown them
with glory and honour.'

As the Divine Logos, now and forever incarnate in Jesus Christ,
had intended in the beginning, Adam and Eve are restored as the
master and mistress of the created world. This is what the marriage crowns express. Here is the beginning of a small kingdom
which can be something like the true kingdom. They then drink a
cup of ordinary wine together to show that even at the simplest
level they are to share each other's lives. They are led in a
circular procession to mark the fact that their union is to last
forever, like the circle without end. The choir sings 'Isaiah rejoice,
the Virgin is with child and will bear a son, and call his name
Emmanuel, God-with-us.' As Jesus was the fruit of the womb of
Mary, the Virgin Israel, sacramental marriage is part of the
mystery of 'God-with-us,' the mystery of Christ and the church.

The Orthodox church, like the Catholic church, does not close
its eyes to the fact that marriages can fail. This is doubly distress-
ing, precisely because of the deep human and sacramental significance that the church attributes to marriage. While the Catholic

church does not allow divorce on the grounds of what God has joined together let no man put asunder (Mark 10:9), the Orthodox church does grant divorce and remarriage on the authority that if a man divorces his wife, *for any cause other than adultery*, and marries another, he commits adultery (Matthew 19:9), understanding by this that Jesus allowed one exception to his general ruling about the indissolubility of marriage.

The Orthodox church in no way encourages divorce and regards the breakdown of marriage as a sin and an evil. But while holding to this, it does not wish the sinner to be placed in an impossible pastoral situation, cut off from the life-giving sacraments. The Orthodox church follows the ancient procedure for the reconciliation of penitents as it is applied to those who marry for a second or third time. If one of the divorced partners eventually intends to begin a new married life, the church will bless this marriage too. The ceremonies for this second marriage, however, are not the same as for the first. In the service for a second marriage several of the joyful prayers and ceremonies are omitted, including the crowning, and a distinctly penitential note is introduced. A third marriage is possible, but a fourth is absolutely forbidden.

In the matter of marriage, divorce and remarriage, it is the bishop who has all authority. This is in line with the Orthodox view that the bishop is 'the apostle in the church.' It is his role to bind and to loose. The East has no equivalent of the Catholic church's marriage tribunals and ecclesiastical courts. The bishop as the *oikonomos* (the one who can intervene to dispense) makes the final act of *philanthropia* (loving kindness) to the ones who have put themselves into an impossible situation vis-à-vis the normative law. Eastern Rite Catholics, who are in union with Rome, follow the law of the Roman church in the matter of divorce and remarriage.

PENANCE

Any sin is a wounding for which healing must be sought. Like all of his gifts, God's healing is found infallibly in the church, since the Holy Spirit has been poured out upon her. The sacrament of Reconciliation is a special sacrament of Christ's healing in the church, and as such, it is related to Baptism, the sacrament which engenders fundamental reconciliation to God and constitutes membership of his body, the church. Reconciliation, therefore, has often been called a 'Second Baptism' in the East, since the sacrament both heals and leads to an experience of *metanoia*, or change of heart. Through praise, prayer, sacramental absolution, spiritual advice and a penance, the sacrament empowers a person to turn to the living God and to turn away from sin and centeredness on one's self.

Following the tradition of the fathers of the church, Eastern theology understands a human being in terms of capacity for freedom. *Metanoia*, the inner turning to God bestowed by reconciliation, is an exercise of this freedom. Strengthened and forgiven, the believer seeks to be restored to growth in the freedom of Christ; to break free of the dehumanizing compulsiveness of sin, whether physical, psychic, mental or spiritual. As baptism bestows a fundamental freedom upon the baptized, reconciliation awakens and extends the freedom of the child of God which is the ability to grow into a mature Christian personality; to become God's glory, which is man fully alive.

When an Eastern Christian goes to confession there are things to do as well as to say. Reconciliation has a clearly visible element of worship. Praise of God is itself a healing. Confessions are therefore almost always heard in the church in front of the icon screen. On a stand are placed a Cross and either an Icon of the Saviour or the Book of Gospels.

As the penitent approaches the stand he invokes the Holy Trinity by making the sign of the Cross. He then kisses the Cross, the source of man's forgiveness, and the Icon or the Gospels, which are presences of the Saviour to whom the confession is being made. The priest emphasizes this in his opening exhortation. Standing alongside the penitent, he says:

> Behold, my child, Christ stands here invisibly and receives your confession. Therefore be not ashamed nor afraid; conceal nothing from me, but tell me without hesitation everything that you have done, and so you shall have pardon from Our Lord Jesus Christ. See, his holy ikon is before us, and I am but a witness, bearing testimony before him of all the things which you have to say to me. But if you conceal anything, you shall have the greater sin. Take heed, therefore, lest, having come to a physician, you depart unhealed.

The penitent then confesses his sins. Sometimes this takes a question and answer form. Sometimes the penitent does it unassisted. Throughout the confession the priest gives advice and direction, which expresses the element of healing. When the confession and advice are concluded, the penitent either bows his head or kneels while the priest places his stole and hands on the penitent's head. This laying on of hands is an important sign. Indeed, it is the sign of the power of the Holy Spirit, by whom sins are forgiven and healing imparted.

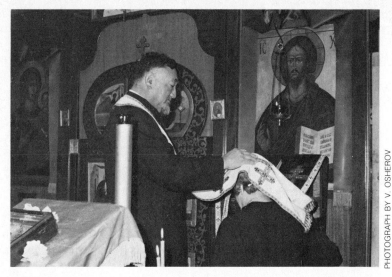

PHOTOGRAPH BY V. OSHEROV

'Repentance is the trembling of the soul before the gates of the kingdom'
(St. Isaac the Syrian).

There are two forms of absolution. One is influenced by the West, containing the 'I forgive and absolve you' phrase. The other is the more deprecative Eastern form, beginning with 'May this same Lord and God, through me a sinner, forgive you.' The second is the more common and we will cite it here. The Russians tend to use the first form, the Greeks use the second.

> The Lord God through Nathan the Prophet forgave David his sin, and the adulteress weeping at his feet, and Peter shedding bitter tears for his betrayal, and the Publican and the Prodigal son. May this same Lord and God, through me a sinner, forgive you, . . . all the sins of your life in this world and in the world to come. And may he make you stand uncondemned at his awesome tribunal, for he is blessed for ever and ever. Amen.[38]

The priest may then suggest a penance. Kissing the Cross, the Icons or the Gospels, as well as the priest's hand, the penitent returns to his place in the congregation to pray the prayers after confession.

There are some variations in the rite according to local usage. In Greece, both priest and penitent often sit. Some places they might sit or stand behind a special screen. In any of these variations, however, the words and gestures are the same. Some Eastern Rite Catholic churches have introduced confessionals which is a departure from Eastern tradition and which takes away from the liturgical nature of the celebration of Reconciliation.

FAST AND FEAST

Until some few years ago, Catholics recognized each other at Saturday night parties as those who stopped eating and drinking as midnight came around. They were also the ones who passed up the meat dishes on Fridays. In those days, if a Catholic really abandoned the faith, among the very first things to be abandoned were fast and abstinence. Although the fasts practiced by the East are longer and much more complex than in the older Catholic style and even though they are not enforced by any compulsion by the church, the very last things to go are the fasts if an Orthodox person begins to slip away from the faith. The ghost of the cycle of fasts, though much attenuated, may continue for years.

The East keeps four main fasts every year. The Great Fast (Lent) begins seven weeks before Easter. The Apostles' Fast is as short as one week or as long as six, depending on the year, leading up to the feasts of St. Peter and St. Paul on June 29. The Assumption Fast is for two weeks leading up to Our Lady's Dormition on August 15 and the Christmas Fast is for forty days before Christmas. Before the reader gasps, there is more. Every Wednesday and Friday of the year are fast days, as are the vigils of the Feast of Epiphany, St. John the Baptist and the Holy Cross.

Fasting in the East is a matter of *what* is eaten. For example, on most days in Great Lent and Holy Week, not only is meat not allowed, but fish and all animal products (such as butter, milk, eggs, cheese), wine and oil are excluded. Naturally conditions of modern life have made it quite difficult for the fasts to be observed in every detail, especially in new countries and climates. Nevertheless, the fasting spirit and practice is still strong, since fasting reveals some of the fundamental everyday attitudes toward life in Christ as it is understood in the East.

One does not fast to punish the body. That would be perversity. Neither is the body evil. That would be heretical. The body is the temple of God. The Spirit of God dwells in the Christian. But from the co-operation of a free being, one with another, the Holy Spirit seeks to draw each man and woman, body and spirit, into an ever deeper share of the life of the Father and the Son. Life in God, after all, is not a matter of the soul alone. The body is also destined for glory, 'yet in my flesh shall I see God.' Fasting is *ascesis*, exercise or discipline. It is not punishment. It is part of the whole man's attempt to open himself to the Holy Spirit. It is not enough for prayer to be of the 'mind,' or for Christian life to be 'mental.' Only when mind and body co-operate in symphony will prayer arise from 'the heart,' a term used in the East, par-

The rich foods of Easter — a sign of Messiah. At this table men and women must be able to say: 'Let us embrace one another. Let us say "brethren" even to those who dislike us, and let us forgive everything in the Resurrection' (St. John of Damascus).

ticularly by St. Gregory Palamas and his school, to indicate the true center of the human person. Fasting is part of the body's symphonic co-operation with the Holy Spirit, an affirmation that Christian life is holistic. Fasting is intended to assist the Christian vision to widen so that all things on earth are seen in their relation to things in heaven. It is also part of *metanoia*, repentance, the reorientation of man's being toward God. While physical fasting sharpens the senses (a natural religious experience, which is not specifically Christian) it can also be an invitation to the love of God to penetrate to the roots of nature and instinct, in order that God may 'change even the substance of things.'[39] Fasting is also a sign of man's unquenchable thirst and continuing hunger for God, which is satisfied by the life-giving Spirit of God in the Eucharist.

While the fasts are severe, feasts are equally exuberant. All the foods from which the believer has abstained throughout Great Lent are blessed in the liturgy of Easter night: meats and cakes, rich breads and eggs. Hallowed in the church, they are eaten with great gusto in the family parties that follow the vigil of Easter. This is a sign of the kingdom, the feast of wisdom. The church and the family are recognized as paradise in which the seasons and all the fruits of nature are God's gift for the delight of man. Through the mystery of Easter, nature and the very life of man are becoming the kingdom. The eggs of Easter, which have been colored and decorated through the week in each family, speak of the new life won for man by Jesus. The families play a game with the eggs, cracking them together, end-to-end. The winner is the holder of the egg that did not shatter. As the eggs crack, the same greeting that filled the whole celebration in church is taken up. One person says 'Christ is risen!' and the other responds, 'He is indeed!' Until the time of Pentecost arrives, this is the way everyone is greeted at any time of the day in Orthodox countries. It replaces 'Good morning' and 'Good evening.' Even in Communist Russia a party member would still begin a party meeting with the words *Christos voskrese* if it is still the Easter season, apparently without noticing that he or she has said anything at all incongruous.

All the major events of life are celebrated with quite a deal of verve in the Eastern church since it is this very world which will enter into the liberty and splendor of the children of God because of Jesus Christ's saving death and resurrection. The world and man can now be legitimately celebrated because of Jesus. The authentic element in paganism has been rescued and transfigured in the Incarnation. The house in which the family lives is regularly blessed by the priest. Festivals for name days and baptisms are

held there. It is the domestic church, in that all the elements that
go to make the Divine Liturgy which is celebrated in the church
or cathedral are drawn from the family. Not only the gifts of
bread and wine, oil and candles, but the worshipper as well.
Baptisms and name day celebrations give us a glimpse of this.

In Greece a baby is baptized between the ages of one and two
years. In many cases the baby remains unnamed until the actual
day of baptism. The baby has only a pet name or is just called
'baby' while the name is worked out and decided upon by parents
and godparents. The child often bears the name of a deceased
relative. In the baptism itself the child's name is revealed for the
first time. The significance is as obvious as it is meaningful.
Customs such as this, however, do not easily carry over into the
new countries.

Eastern Christians ignore birthdays almost entirely and celebrate
each person's name day. This is a day when preparations begin
early in the home. All sorts of foods are cooked and the house is
decorated. The person whose name day it is dresses up especially
well and attends the liturgy with the family and friends. At the
end of the liturgy, during which the person being celebrated
received Communion, the priest will conduct an office (prayer
service) in honor of their saint. The feast days of saints such as
St. Constantine, St. Helen, St. George and St. Nicholas are great
celebrations in the Greek church.[40] The parties that follow the
services are likely to go on all night, with lots of handshaking,
kissing and the greeting 'many years!'

CHAPTER FOUR

Tradition in Life

EARTH MADE HEAVEN

The mystery of the Incarnation, God's coming among us as a man in Jesus Christ, governs the Eastern church's attitude to the created world and to the nature of Christian worship in the world. When the church prays, most particularly in the Divine Liturgy, heaven and earth are in communion.

> Let us, who here mystically represent the Cherubim in singing the thrice-holy hymn to the life-giving Trinity, lay aside every earthly care. (Hymn of the Great Entrance)

Through the obedient and loving worship of men and women, the whole of the creation is reoriented to reveal the mystery and glory of God. The church is revealed as paradise, the environment in which man and the whole of creation speak of God and point to the divine. The arrangement of the church, its architecture, furnishings and decoration, as well as what takes place in it, speak of the mystery of the divine – human communion manifest in time, of communion with the Father, through Jesus Christ, in the Spirit. With the patriarch Jacob, the church says, 'God is in this place.' In the Holy Liturgy the church recognizes herself in Jacob's words, 'This is nothing less than a house of God; this is the gate of heaven' (Genesis 28:17).

Orthodox churches are most often square in shape and are distinctive for their one or many domes. The dome signifies the descent of the Holy Spirit upon creation, his transforming of the material world by his redeeming power. The interior of the church is richly decorated with icons and frescoes. During the services it is ablaze with candles and lamps. It is filled with the sweet smoke of incense. It resounds with the singing of the service and is alive with the movements of the clergy and people. It is the transfigured earth which has glimpsed heavenly light and fire, reflecting it in design, color, movement, smell and sound.[41]

What would be called the sanctuary in the West is screened off from the main body of the church by an icon screen, or iconostasis. It is a wall pierced by three sets of doors. The center double doors are often called the Holy Doors or the Royal Doors. The side doors are called the north (left) and the south (right) door. These lesser doors get their names from the tradition of earlier days which required that churches be built facing the east, 'from whence came our salvation.' The deacon uses the south door and the servers use the north door. Only the clergy use the central doors, the one exception being the emperor who, in ancient days, was given the honor, as protector of the Christian people, of entering the Holy Doors to receive Communion in the sanctuary.

A Byzantine church built in 1030 at Samtavisi, Georgia (Christian in the fourth century). Some of the most beautiful Orthodox churches ever built stand derelict or secularised today, owing to the savage persecutions waged against the Georgian church.

Laymen never enter the sanctuary, except for serving the liturgy. Even then, no one except the priest or bishop should ever pass in front of the Holy Table or Throne.[42] Servers and others must pass behind it.

In a Byzantine church the altar is a square table which stays well away from the walls. The sacred ceremonies cannot be

The interior of the Church of St. George, Gelati, Georgia.

properly carried out if the priest and deacon cannot move freely around the altar. Only the sacred ministers ever touch the altar. On the altar an *antimension* is used instead of the Catholic practice of having an altar stone. This is a square piece of cloth bearing a representation of the taking-down of Jesus from the Cross. Relics of the saints are sewn inside it. Also on the altar is a tabernacle for the reservation of the blessed sacrament (often a miniature of a church) and the richly decorated Book of the Gospels.

Behind the tabernacle there is a branched lamp stand upon which
up to seven lamps burn during the liturgy.

The iconostasis (the screen) is decorated with many sacred
images or icons. The proscribed icons are that of Our Lord on
the right of the central doors, with that of Our Lady on the left.
A representation of the Last Supper is usually placed over the
Royal Doors. Icons of the Archangels, Gabriel and Michael, as
well as the holy deacons, St. Stephen and St. Lawrence, are
usually placed on the north and south doors, or in positions close
to them. The icon screen is a reminder of the separation between
God and man. But God has entered the world to end that
separation. To mark this, the screen is pierced by doors, as we
have explained. When the doors are opened (in many churches
now they remain open for the whole of the service) the altar can
be seen in the center of the sanctuary, a symbol of God's throne
and of his glory.[43]

The Royal Doors open onto the throne of Glory, while the way
they are decorated further reveals the meaning of this symbol.
The doors almost always portray the four evangelists, by whose
inspired writings the heart of man is opened in faith and repentance to the life-giving Spirit, and thus to the grace of the
mystery of Incarnation, the person of Jesus who, in his own
person, ends man's separation from God. The doors also portray
the Annunciation, the very moment of the wonder of the Incarnation's realization. Taken as a whole, the doors represent Christ
who is the living opening to the heavenly sanctuary of the divine
nature: Christ, through whom man is drawn to the Father.

We have spent some time on this one feature of the church to
demonstrate that the placing of icons is not arbitrary. The icons,
frescoes and mosaics are not mere ornaments designed to make
the church look nice. They have a theological and liturgical
function. The icons are meeting points of heaven and earth;[44]
realizations of the saints and of the mysteries which they portray.

> ... these visible images remind the faithful unceasingly of the invisible
> presence of the whole company of heaven at the liturgy [and] they are
> helped to realise that their Liturgy on earth is one and the same with
> the great Liturgy of heaven ... ikons express visibly the sense of
> heaven on earth.[45]

The Byzantine liturgy[46] engages all the senses of the worshipper. Believing that 'man is above all else a liturgical being who is
most truly himself when he glorifies God,'[47] the gleaming iconostasis portrays the household of heaven, our true home. The
solemn processions, the deacon's ministry of prayer between
people and sanctuary, and the resounding doxologies, give 'all

praise and honor and glory' to the Persons of the Most Holy Trinity. A sacred atmosphere is evoked in incense, lights and song, and the frequent litanies which beg God's blessing on all mankind and on all his works. These create the context which best demonstrates the Byzantine church's sacramental realism.

Two prayers, dramatic in their directness, demonstrate the reality that becomes the sacred ethos of the liturgy. The first from the Great Entrance of the Gift prays:

> It is to You, then, that I come with my Head bowed low ... I beg You, do not exclude me from the number of Your children, but rather allow these gifts to be offered to You by me, Your sinful and unworthy servant. For it is really You who offer and are offered, You who receive the offering and are given back to us, Christ our God....

The second, which reveals the Eucharist as the sustenance of all life, comes shortly after the Lord's Prayer. It tells us that the worshippers

> do not bow before flesh and blood, but before You, their awe-inspiring God. Therefore, O Lord, distribute to all of us for our own good and according to each one's needs, the gifts that lie here before us. Sail with those on the sea, journey with all travellers, care for the sick, O Lord, healer of souls and bodies.

The church, its furnishings and all that happens there, particularly the Holy Eucharist, transport the believer into the eternal world of God. It is a place in this world, but not of the world. It is the 'gate of heaven' and 'Yahweh is in this place' (Genesis 28:16−17). Time is suspended. Indeed, 'a day in your courts,' sang David, 'is better than a thousand elsewhere.' Liturgical time suspends the inexorable and tyrannous flow of earthly time, giving access to the 'now' of eternity where God is all in all, and where man (mind, senses, body and heart) is caught up into God and receives his true nature, that of worshipping man.

THE WORSHIPPER IN THE CHURCH

There is a legend which throws light upon the nature of Orthodox worship and its relationship to the faith. It comes from the first days of the conversion of Kievan Russia. Its first Christian king, Vladimir, the prince of Kiev, while still a pagan, wished to know whether he should embrace Islam or Christianity. He sent envoys to see how the Muslims worshipped in Bulgaria, to Germany and to Rome, and of course, to Constantinople, capital of the Byzantine world. The envoys thought Islam was all words and quite joyless. They were impressed by Catholic worship in Rome, but found their services rather restrained. In Constantinople, however, they found what they were seeking.

> We did not know whether we were in heaven or on earth, for surely there is no splendour or beauty anywhere upon earth. We cannot describe it to you; only this we know, that there God dwells amongst men and their service surpasses the worship of all other places. For we cannot forget that beauty.[48]

They adopted the Byzantine tradition of worship, which is to say, the Eastern Christian approach to the faith. They chose it, paradoxically, not because it is lofty and spiritual, but precisely because it is so earthly and tangible. 'We cannot forget that beauty.' It moved their hearts by touching their senses. Byzantine Christianity is not other-worldly. Rather, it places the strongest emphasis upon 'this' world as the place in which the Unknowable God makes himself known. Because of Jesus Christ, the New Adam, the fallen world of creation, the world of matter and time, is being restored as a bearer of the divine meaning and presence. God approaches man through the elements of this world, his very approach filling time and matter with a new beauty, God's beauty. The worship of the East shows that the Incarnation has altered reality. Far from being lofty and mystical in the worst sense, Byzantine worship is realist, showing that only what is oriented upon the Incarnation is truly real. Just before the singing of the Nicene Creed (the Christian vision of the true nature of divine and human reality) the priest and deacon give each other the kiss of peace, one saying 'Let Christ be among us' and the other responding 'He both is and will be.'

A Byzantine Christian is not a mere spectator at a solemn show. The Byzantine liturgy is a popular liturgy. Although most of the singing is done by the choir, it is in a language known to the worshipper. The East has always used the common languages from the very beginning. It would be a mistake to think that the role of the choir takes away from that of the people. It is really the same thing. Perhaps it would be better to see the choir's service as one which allows the worshipper to follow the liturgy inwardly, and perhaps more closely than if he had to sing throughout.

Many other features as well as the language and the singing reveal the popular nature of Eastern worship. There are very few seats in the churches, which allows the congregation to move about if so desired. Standing freely grouped together creates an atmosphere of freedom in the face of God, which neat pews and regimented rows make difficult. Let us follow Eastern Christians into the church and watch what they are likely to do.

'*I worship the Creator of matter, who for my sake became material and deigned to dwell in matter, who through matter effected my salvation*' (St. John of Damascus).

*The Book of the Holy Gospels, Russia, early
seventeenth century.*

First of all, you will find that they are not obsessive about arriving on time, nor will a priest ever embarrass people about such a thing. The liturgy is a long service, often preceded by Matins (as in the Greek church), consequently the worshippers pick up the service or allow themselves to be absorbed by it whenever they arrive. The East's attitude to public worship contrasts strongly to that of the West. People enter the liturgy, as into a divine atmosphere, while the West tends to think of each person subjectively bringing something to common worship.

At the door of the church they will buy some candles and a small loaf of bread, *prosphora*. This is taken by a server into the sanctuary along with a list of that person's friends and relatives for whom it is wished to pray during the liturgy. The priest will cut a small piece from the loaf and place this piece upon the paten. During the liturgy, and just before Communion time, this

The Panagia (All Holy One), a pectoral icon worn
by the bishops of the Eastern churches.

piece of bread, representing those for whom we wish to pray, the
living and the dead, will be mixed with the consecrated wine. It is
a sign of divinization. The blessed but unconsecrated bread is
soaked utterly in the blood of Christ. The lists are used throughout the liturgy to pray for these people by name. At the end of
the liturgy the worshipper receives back the bread from which
was taken the piece that was mixed with the precious blood. It is
eaten reverently by the family at home.

On going into the church the worshipper approaches the Icon
of the Feast which is set up in a place of honor in the middle of
the church. Making a sign of the Cross,[49] the worshipper kisses
the icon and sometimes makes a *metany* (profound bow), touching
the floor with the right hand. One of the candles will be lit and
placed here. The worshipper then moves freely around the church

*The Holy Chalice, Kremlin Workshops, Moscow,
1598.*

greeting the icons of Our Lady and Jesus in the same way. There
is really no set order. Each person may well go to reverence
particular saints for whom there is a special devotion, lighting
candles in their honor as he or she pauses before each one. The
worshipper will then go and stand wherever desired among the
people, usually greeting and kissing friends.

One will not find people with their heads buried in books in an
Orthodox church, as it limits the worshipper's field of vision and
closes the senses to the liturgy's revelation of the relationship of
things earthly and heavenly. There is no need of books, for the
worshipper knows the public parts of the liturgy from childhood.

*The Paten and Diskos, Kremlin Workshops,
Moscow, late seventeenth century.*

Nor is there anything very studied or self-conscious about the
way Eastern Christians worship. Each person can respond in
many ways to parts of the service which move him. The sign of
the Cross is made constantly throughout the liturgy. Every mention
of the Holy Trinity is greeted this way. Often people bow and
cross themselves, and sometimes they use the more profound
bow, or *metany*. With the palm of the right hand turned upward,
the worshipper lowers the hand to the floor, making a deep bow
with the whole body. These movements are not studied. One
makes them when one wishes to as a kind of sacred emphasis.
People move about, sometimes to pray before an icon, and in
some churches at the entrance of the Gospels many go to kiss the
Scriptures as they are carried in procession.

As the liturgy unfolds it is as if time is suspended. In this timelessness the Byzantine church unfolds its essential movement in a
systematic and logical rhythm. The liturgy develops from the humble
listening of the catchumen to the welcoming of Christ in his Gospel
(Liturgy of the Word), then to oblation, intercession, adoration,
consecration (Offertory and Eucharistic Prayer) and finally to

transformation into Christ through contact with him (Communion). At every point in this unfolding of the mysteries of the life of Jesus, theology is expressed in the warmest and most poetic of terms and is enhanced further by the music. Nothing is ever said in the Byzantine church, with the exception of this prayer before Holy Communion. In its setting, this must surely be one of the most powerful prayers that one is ever likely to hear. When the time for Communion arrives the priest faces the congregation. Holding the chalice he prays:

> Receive me today, O Son of God, as a participant in your mystical supper; for I shall not betray your sacrament to your enemies, nor give you a kiss like Judas, but like the thief I will acknowledge you. Remember me, Lord, in your kingdom.

It is impossible to mistake what the Christian of the East believes about the Eucharist.

MONASTICISM

A monk is someone who is alone (*monos*) — a Christian who goes apart, who is set apart in the church to pattern his life on Christ, most particularly on the Christ who was tempted by the devil in the wilderness. A monk's vows of poverty, chastity and obedience correspond to the three temptations of Jesus as described in the Gospel (Luke 4:1 – 13). As St. Gregory Palamas noted, 'They (the monks) have renounced the rewards of material goods (poverty), human glory (obedience) and the evil pleasures of the body (chastity), and they have preferred an evangelical life; thus the perfect have arrived at the adult age according to Christ.'[50] As such, a monk is a rebel, God's rebel, whose life is a sign and a prophecy. To his fellow believers in the church, a monk's life is a sign of the realization of the kingdom of God. To the values of profane society, a monk's life is not marginal. Rather, it stands at the very center of Christianity and it has everything to do with the modern world. The monastic life proclaims that goodness, beauty and truth are the true standards of value, and not efficiency, material success, power or force. Like the prophets of the Old Testament, the monk's life preaches adoration of the one God, purification of the people and the exercise of charity toward the poor.[51] A monk's life is the evangelical life or the 'good news' life, since it is Jesus and the power of his Holy Spirit who has made it possible for men and women to live in this new, authentically human way.

Monasticism stands at the very heart of the life of the Eastern church but, unlike the West, the East does not have religious orders. There are no equivalents of Dominicans, Christian Brothers or Jesuits. The monasteries, convents and hermitages spread throughout the Orthodox world constitute a monastic order: a monastic way of life, but not in any monolithic sense. Each monastery is an independent entity, with its own atmosphere. Men or women do not become monks or nuns for only a period of their lives. They choose to be so for life.

It may puzzle a Western Catholic to be told that monasticism still retains a lay character in the East. What of the black robes, communities, long services, great fasts and the intense life of prayer? Are these not the marks of the clergyman? Are not monks priests? The answer in both cases is no. Most monks are not priests, although some are in holy orders to minister to the sacramental life of their fellows. A man does not enter a monastery to become a priest or deacon. A consideration of the origins of monastic life will show us the essential function of the monk and the nun in the East, and that the ancient patterns and purpose of monastic life continue, with some modifications, to our own day and should not be confused with priesthood.

Monasticism arose in the period of the cessation of persecution by the Roman state. Or, put in another way, in the period when it became respectable to be a Christian. Despite the wonder of St. Constantine's conversion, the new safety was in some ways highly dangerous. Many ordinary Christians feared that new privilege could lead to decadence. They felt called to go apart from the world as witnesses. The monks and nuns were to be what the martyrs had previously been. They were attempting to take seriously Paul's injunction that if the times are evil then by the holiness of his life, by his strivings, such as fasting, and by intense and ceaseless prayer, the Christian must attempt to redeem the times. Monasticism is clearly not an adjunct to the Christian life. It is the witness to the faith, the eschatological[52] sign of the kingdom of God in time, in the midst of the church. As the martyr is in the church and is a witness to it, so is the monk and the nun.

In the days of monasticism's birth in the East, some men and women went to live as hermits in the solitude of the great deserts of Egypt and Palestine where they prayed for the church and the world. Others came together in communities, often gathered around a particularly wise and holy elder, and pursued the same work of prayer and intercession. From the very beginning, the Christian people valued these athletes of the spirit and streamed to their communities to be refreshed in the community's prayer

The Monastery of Simonopetra (Simon's rock), Mount Athos, founded in the fourteenth century.

and to seek spiritual advice and direction from those charismatic individuals who had received the gift of spiritual insight. St. Anthony the Great, father of Eastern monasticism, was the first of these elders or spiritual fathers — *geronda* in Greek; *starets* in Russian.[53]

Orthodox people still turn to the monks for spiritual direction, often in a life-long relationship. In new countries such as Canada or the United States or Australia, this can be difficult, as there are few monks, but it is still something to which devout Orthodox look forward.

The greatest center of Orthodox monastic life is Mount Athos, *Agion Oros*, the Holy Mountain, a rocky peninsula in northern Greece, which at one time was the home to some 40,000 monks. It is made up of some twenty major monasteries and many smaller houses and hermitages. To visit Athos on pilgrimage is a hope possible only for devout Orthodox men. Women are never allowed there. Athos is a place remarkable for its physical beauty, as well as for its quality of timelessness.

All of the various styles of monastic life are found on Athos. There are three basic styles. The first, which looks to St. Anthony as its founder, is the life of the hermit, the man of solitary prayer (eremitic). The second, which looks to St. Pachomius, is a style of community life under a common rule (cenobitic). This was the style that was to influence St. Benedict when he began his monasteries in the West. The third style stands between the first two and for this reason it is called the semi-eremitical, semi-hermit or middle way (idiorrhythmic). This style is quite as ancient as the way of the hermits and the community system. In fact Irish monasteries followed something like this style of life before the era of the Benedictines. Monasteries of the middle way are more loosely organized groups of small settlements (*sketes*), each containing a handful of monks under the guidance of an elder.

Eastern monasticism is considered to be pre-eminently practical. Like sacramental marriage, it is the Christian life in *praxis*, in action. The East does not see any split between contemplation and action, between prayer and work. Rather, contemplation is a good work, if not the pre-eminent good work. Consequently, to work is to pray, to pray is to work. St. Benedict and St. Anthony are in complete concord here, since both believe that Christian life is reality itself, not some sort of religious allegory.

Eastern mysticism is not vague or dreamy. It is specific and doctrinally centered. The mystic is not one who begins the life of contemplation by pondering nature or the cosmos. The gaze of the Christian mystic is fixed on Jesus Christ, in whose person man and creation are restored to communion with God. The love of mankind and the creation are thus authentically restored to the mystic by the Holy Spirit of Jesus. As the very ground of all earthly and spiritual reality, only Christ can disclose the secrets of the world's restoration.

Somewhere in the writings of Nikos Katzantzakis there is a story that he tells of an encounter with an old monk on Mount Athos. As a layman on pilgrimage, he came upon the old monk whose face streamed with tears as he gazed at a leaf which he held in his hand. 'Why are you weeping?' the traveler asked.

'Having once put your foot on the ladder on which God had leaned, do not cease to go up ... each rung leads to the one beyond' (St. Gregory of Nyssa). *Icon from St. Katherine's Monastery, Mount Sinai.*

'Because I see Christ crucified,' replied the elder. No sooner
had he said this, he turned over the leaf. His old face lit up with
joy.
'Why are you smiling, Father?' asked the traveler.
'Because I see Jesus in the glory of his resurrection.'
Eastern monasticism begins with attention to God in prayer. It
does not begin with the contemplation of the leaf.

The monks of the East have made interventions in the life of
the church, as well as other contributions, without which Orthodoxy
would not be its true self. In the seventh and eighth centuries, the
monks defended one of Orthodoxy's most distinctive features,
the theology and veneration of icons. In the fourteenth century,
they both defended and extended the teaching of the Jesus Prayer
(Prayer of the Heart) which, like the icons, stands at the very
center of Eastern Orthodoxy's approach to the divine–human
mystery. Finally, almost all of the services which the everyday
believer attends were enriched in the monasteries. One author
has written that the Orthodox monk, and most particularly the
elder, is one who is called to withdraw from the world, so that
God, if he wills it, may return him to it. History clearly demonstrates that the monastic estate has performed this role in the life
of the church, just as the saintly elders have performed it in the
individual lives of their spiritual children.

ICONS

An icon is a religious picture (from the Greek for 'image') which
represents Christ, Our Lady, the saints and angels, or the mysteries of the Christian faith. Along with the Holy Cross, icons play a
very prominant role in the devotional and liturgical life of Eastern
Christians. They are neither idols nor objects of art. They are a
way in which one enters the world of heaven. They are a means
by which that reality is made present in life. Potentially they
express the redemption of mankind and the restoration and transfiguration of the fallen world. An icon can be as small and
portable as an egg tempera painting on a piece of wood, or as
large as a fresco or mosaic on the walls of a great church.

Icons are suddenly fashionable. Most book stores of any size
will have something on their shelves to do with this or that school
of iconography or with the icons of various countries and regions.
Icons also appear more often in antique collections and among
the Picassos and prints on the walls of middle-class homes. To
find an icon treated as an interesting object or merely as a
painting, saddens the Eastern Christian. Icons are not pictures

like any other. To treat them so offends the deepest sensibilities of the East.

No home could be Orthodox, let alone fervent, without its icons; images of the Saviour, Our Lady, the saints and the mysteries of the Christian faith. The icon is the bearer of a presence to the believer, not the reminder of an absence. Its place in the church and in the home is sacramental. Daily life without this presence would seem very odd indeed to the Eastern Christian mentality.

The icons are placed in a position of honor in the home (often in the corner of a room) and a lamp burns before them. People pray before the icons, in what the Russians call 'the glowing corner,' using the same gestures as in church, the sign of the Cross, deep bows and prostrations. During their prayer incense is burned before the icons. It is a sign of a sacramental presence and a sign of prayer. When a family recites the grace before meals, they don't join hands or bow heads around the table. They turn and face the icons. As evening comes on, people light the lamps before the icons and incense the rooms of the house, a sign that the Christian home is the domestic church, a place where God is present to man.

Eastern Christianity reverences the icons because they are a way of access, along with the Scriptures, into the mystery of the Incarnation, the mystery of Christ. In him, man is remade in the image of God. Creation is restored to its true nature, manifesting Divinity.

> O Lord, wishing to fulfill that which You had ordained from eternity, You have received ministers from all of the creation at this, Your mystery: Gabriel from among the angels, the Virgin from among men, the Star from the heavens and the Jordan from among the waters. (Compline of Theophany)

Because of its attention to the mystery of the Incarnation, Byzantine Christianity gives the fullest emphasis to matter and time, because it is in them that God has manifested himself. In the Matins of the Feast of the Theophany, the river Jordan is given a voice. It cries out, 'I have seen him naked who cannot be seen, and I trembled.' God has made matter spirit-bearing. Flesh has become a vehicle of the Spirit. So then, though in a different way, have wood and paint.

> Keeping the laws of the Church that we have received from the Fathers, we paint icons of Christ and His saints, and with our lips and hearts, we will venerate them as we cry aloud: O all ye works of the Lord, bless Ye the Lord! (Eighth Canticle of the Matins of Orthodox Sunday)

The Harrowing of Hell, from a fourteenth-century fresco in the Chora Monastery, Constantinople.

The East has no time for puritan approaches to worship — that tendency to cry idolatry at the first hint of beauty in song, image or liturgy. It is a tendency latent in many Christians, although it has no place in Christianity itself. In 843 at the last council which both Catholic and Orthodox recognize as ecumenical in status, scope and authority, the whole church, the Romans of the West and the East, condemned the denigrators of images, the breakers of icons,[54] as heretics.

The East celebrates this Triumph of Orthodoxy on the first Sunday of Lent. It is the Feast of the Icons; the feast of all beauty, of the restored creation.

> Restoring to the churches the representations of Your flesh, O Lord, we give them an honor that is relative, and so express the great mystery of Your dispensation. For You have not appeared to us, O Lover of Mankind, merely in an outward appearance, as say the followers of Mani, who are enemies of God,[55] but in the full and true reality of the flesh, and so the icons that depict Your flesh lead us to the desire and love of Thee. (Ninth Canticle of the Vespers of Orthodox Sunday)

An icon is not merely a painting, it is a work of prayer and theology. Likewise, the artists are not simply painters. They are theologians. Only someone living in the Tradition can make a genuine icon. The artist prepares for the work with prayer and fasting. When finished, the icon is taken to the church, placed on the Holy Table in the sanctuary along with the Gospels, where it is hallowed by prayer and by its immersion in the liturgy. Sometimes it is anointed with oil and sprinkled with holy water before it takes its place in the church or in the home.[56] The icon teaches the faith to all the senses.

Perhaps a brief exposition of a particular icon could best explain icons as works of prayer and theology and their role as a locus of faith. The Icon of the Descent into Hell (the Harrowing of Hell) is one of the favorite themes in Eastern Christian art. After his passion and death Jesus descended into hell to free the dead from death. The icon shows Jesus in a mandala of light: 'Thou hast slain hell with the dazzling light of thy divinity' (Matins of Holy Saturday). As in the Transfiguration scenes, the human nature of Jesus shows forth God. The figure of Jesus is larger than the other figures in the icon. His presence is commanding and masterful. 'Put to death according to the flesh, He delivers the dead from the grasping hand of hell' (Matins of Holy Saturday). The figure of Jesus is surrounded by the countless figures of all those men and women of the past who awaited his coming — 'how overflowing is the gladness that You have brought to those in hell, shining as lightning in its gloomy depths' (Matins of Holy Saturday). The doors of the underworld are shattered. Locks, keys and chains lie scattered. 'Today hell groans and cries aloud: My power is destroyed. I accepted a mortal man as one of the dead; yet I cannot keep him prisoner ... I held in my power the dead from all ages; but see, He is raising them all' (Vespers of Holy Saturday).

In the forefront of the picture are the figures of Adam and Eve, their hands extended to Jesus, his hands extended to them. 'O my Maker, Thou hast brought to pass the recreation of Eve. Becoming Adam, Thou hast in ways surpassing nature slept a life-giving sleep' (Matins of Holy Saturday). In the gestures of the hands the icon focuses upon the heart of the mystery of redemption in a way that is difficult to put into words. The very God from whom our aboriginal ancestors fled into death has come to find them, to return them to paradise, to union with him. Jesus Christ is this very God from true God, yet through Mary this very God is their descendent in the flesh. Words fail but the image holds the truth before the senses. Icons are not 'holy pictures.' They are visions of the reality found in Scripture and Liturgy. As St. John of Damascus said in their defense: 'The icon is a song of triumph and a revelation; an enduring monument to the victory of the Saints. They are the disgrace of demons.'

Of course, it is Jesus who is the disgrace of the demons and of those who collude with them. Christ, the Divine Light (John 1:9 – 14), shows the counterfeit and shabby nature of the demonic world, of the darkness. It is Jesus, the man who possesses (by his own right) the fullness of divine being and life, who reveals Satan's life and being as a nothing, a self-idol, a metaphysical parasite, a liberty that has failed and become malevolent being. Jesus accomplishes this because he is the very image (icon) of the invisible God (Colossians 1:15). The demons are therefore disgraced by every saint, by every man and woman who lives in Christ, those who, being reformed in Christ's image, embody the divine life in prayer and philanthropy. This is also true of spirit-bearing matter. 'The entire visible world, as depicted in the icon, is to foreshadow the coming unity of the whole creation, of the kingdom of the Holy Spirit,'[57] from which all the illusions and ugliness of the demonic realm are expunged and nullified. The icon is the 'symbol,' the concretization of this certainty.

THE JESUS PRAYER

Since the earliest days of the desert monastic communities the Jesus Prayer, in various forms, has been in use in the East. Both Diadochus of Photice in the fifth century and St. John Climacus in the sixth to seventh centuries recommend the constant remembrance and repetition of the name of Jesus. The prayer became a sentence: 'Lord Jesus Christ, Son of God, have mercy on me, a sinner.' It spread beyond the monasteries and penetrated into the daily lives of believers. It is one of Orthodoxy's most popular prayer forms, suitable for mystics and beginners, for the monastic solitude or when waiting for the bus. Orthodox people often use a cloth rosary, very similar to the Western rosary, for the recitation of the prayer.

St. Paul insistently taught that Christians are those who invoke the name of Jesus Christ (1 Colossians 1:2). He also made it clear that divine power rested in the name of Jesus, such that 'all beings in the heavens, on earth and in the underworld, should bend the knee at the name of Jesus and that every tongue should acclaim Jesus Christ as Lord, to the glory of God the Father' (Philippians 2:10 – 11). The Jesus Prayer, as practiced by the Eastern Christian, steps off with St. Paul's teaching as its foundation, as well as from St. Paul's admonition to pray without ceasing.

The method of the prayer is very simple. The person who prays it says, barely audibly: 'Lord Jesus Christ, Son of God, have

*A sixth-century icon of Jesus, from St. Katherine's
Monastery, Mount Sinai.*

mercy on me, a sinner.' As he (or she) does so, he focuses his
mind's whole attention upon the heart and becomes conscious of
its rhythm. As he becomes more practiced, he also attunes the
prayer to the rhythm of the heart. He also breathes the prayer as
he says it, breathing in the first phrases, breathing out the second
phrases. A rosary of cloth beads is also used to mark each
invocation of the Holy Name. The elements of the Jesus Prayer
concentrate all of one's senses upon the holy task. Such attention
is mastered only by attentive labor, time and divine assistance.
To learn it authentically one also needs an experienced guide or
director. However, the effects of the Jesus Prayer are profound
and wonderful. The writings of the Pilgrim, later referred to, can
best explain those effects.

Unlike a devotion like the rosary, the Jesus Prayer has a more
developed theology. It is necessary to give here at least a simple
outline of this theology, if the sympathetic reader is to understand
the East's approach to sanctification (most often called 'deification'
or *theosis*) or the Eastern approach to the nature of man's communion with God.

We must first understand that

> Orthodox believe that the power of God is present in the Name of
> Jesus, so that the invocation of the Divine Name acts 'as an effective
> sign of God's action, as a sort of sacrament.' 'The Name of Jesus'
> present in the human heart, communicates to it the power of deification
> ... shining through the heart, the light of the Name of Jesus illumi-
> nates all the Universe.[58]

A spirituality which is an imitation of Christ has no great
following in the East. Christianity is life *in* Christ, a life that is
not merely metaphorical. It is in Christ that a true communion
with God is made possible. Jesus Christ is our communion in
God. Christian life, therefore, is not a training ground or a
preparation for a reality to come. There is nothing to continue in
eternity if one is not in Christ in this life. In the sacraments,
Scriptures, prayer and every good work, the Christian puts on
and grows in 'the new self that has been created in God's way'
(Ephesians 4:24). To be a Christian means to be a participant in
the divine—human communion, which is engendered in the soul
by the waters of baptism. The Jesus Prayer is to be understood in
this light. It calls upon Jesus, who himself is the divine—human
communion. Sinful man, who cannot even draw near to God the
Infinite, calls upon Jesus, God-in-the flesh, to bestow his supreme
mercy which is communion with the Unknowable, experience of
the Incomprehensible One, true communion with God, to be a
partaker of the divine nature (2 Peter 1:4).

A nun praying the Jesus Prayer in a Russian church.

St. Gregory Palamas (1296–1359), Archbishop of Thessaloniki, is one of the most important figures in the matter of the Jesus Prayer, and for that matter, in the whole question of *how* one knows God in the life of prayer. St. Gregory agreed with both the Scriptures and the fathers when he said that God cannot be known in his 'essence.' Only God knows himself in his own essence, but God has truly revealed himself in his divine *energies*, which are not separate from God, but in which God exists complete and entire.[59] Knowledge of God in his energies is thus a 'direct' knowledge of God. His energies are God himself, not some secondhand experience or knowledge. Grace is not merely a gift of God, a thing, a quantity or, worse still, a form of credit in a system of spiritual banking. Grace is God himself in communion with man. St. Gregory in the fourteenth century clearly heard the cry of the fifth-century Patriarch of Constantinople, St. John Chrysostom, who told his hearers, 'Never forget that God has made you his friend.' What sort of friendship could this be, if one could never truly know the divine Friend? St. Gregory is a theologian of the divine–human friendship, which is sustained in the life of prayer.

St. Gregory's theology flowered further in the writings of disciples. The most important of these disciples was Nicholas Cabasilas, a layman and public servant. His two books, still available and in English, are *A Commentary on the Divine Liturgy* and *My Life in Christ*. They are both beautifully written and simple, but are also classics for approaching both the characteristic sacramental understanding of the East and the nature of the spiritual life. That they are by an Orthodox layman might make them even more interesting for the lay Western reader.

There is another book, also by a layman, and a very humble man indeed, called *The Way of the Pilgrim*.[60] It is by far the best introduction to the workings and nature of the Jesus Prayer and it is in the form of an account of one man's experience of the prayer. The author was an anonymous Russian peasant of no education, yet he was a master of insight. It is strongly recommended, both because it sets out the steps to be taken to enter the way of prayer and because it describes the effects of the prayer in great detail. Its final charm is that it is utterly simple and free of all pretensions.

CHAPTER FIVE

Eastern Christianity, Today and Tomorrow

THE ORTHODOX CHURCH TODAY

The Orthodox Church is made up of some fourteen autocephalous (self-headed) or self-governing churches. Among these are four of the ancient Patriarchates: Constantinople, Alexandria, Antioch and Jerusalem.[61] Other churches are headed by the new Patriarchates of Moscow, Serbia, Rumania and Bulgaria, the majority of whose populations are Orthodox. Though not new Patriarchates, three other churches belong to this group, going back even to Byzantine times. These are the church of Greece (governed by a Primate and Synod), the church of Cyprus, and the very ancient and much-persecuted church of Georgia, whose head is the Catholicos — Patriarch of Georgia.

Three other churches, though linked to all other centers of authority and administration, are also autocephalous. These are the churches of Albania, Poland and Czechoslovakia, where the Orthodox are a minority in the total population. Other large populations, such as in Australia, Canada or the United States, are not separate churches and are still linked to older centers. The Greek Orthodox church in Australia, for example, with some 700,000 people in 1985, is part of the Patriarchate of Constantinople, as is the United States, Canada and Great Britain. The tiniest Orthodox church of all is the autocephalous monastery of St. Katherine in Sinai.

The structure and organization of the Orthodox church is not utterly fixed. History has shown it to have a capacity for development in accord with circumstances, times and needs. In the new countries the future may show a uniting of jurisdictions to form a single jurisdiction. There are moves in this direction in the United States, where an American Orthodox church has been formed, mainly by members of various Russian jurisdictions. Using American English as its language of worship and preaching it seeks to pursue a more indigenous 'Orthodoxy, suitable to the new situation.' Although such a course presents enormous difficulties and dangers, this must be the direction of the future in the new lands.

When the Byzantine liturgy prays 'for the well-being of the holy Churches of God and the union of all' (Litany of Peace) it does not, in the first instance, mean the large organizational units. The holy church of God is the diocese, the faithful gathered around its bishop. This is the irreducible unit of the church. The pastoral and practical needs of each diocese are ministered to in the parishes of the diocese by priests and deacons placed among the people by the bishop. Most of these parochial clergy are married men in the East. The bishop, however, is never married.

The bishops are all each other's equal. So are the churches, whether ancient or new.

As one would expect, the situation of the Orthodox church in the modern world shares many common features with that of the Catholic church. It also has some unique features, challenges and difficulties, which we will shortly consider. As for the development of mutual understanding between Catholicism and Orthodoxy, one must note a certain lopsidedness. The Orthodox are very critical and attentive to developments in Catholic pastoral practice, but they know very little of Catholic theology. Catholics are almost the reverse. A keen interest in Eastern Christian theology and patristics is much in evidence but knowledge of Eastern Christian pastoral practice is woefully poor. These imbalances need to be rectified if the churches are to face the future together. The International Orthodox/Catholic dialogue, at present being conducted, may go a long way toward this rectification.

On the level of theological life the Orthodox world faces a number of urgent but related tasks. There is a deep need for an authentic return to the 'mind' of the fathers of the church. The church must relearn to reflect and act with the mind of patristic tradition. The fathers need to speak to the whole church once again. Their thoughts, especially their homiletics, need to be made accessible through modern translations and form the basis for all lay activity, both for spiritual growth and for social involvement. In order to do this the church must study, using tools of modern scholarship, the wealth of patristic tradition and not just 'selected' fathers, such as those of the desert. The training of Orthodox theologians needs to proceed from the outcome of this deepened study, by Orthodox for Orthodox, and not from foreign models from outside the Orthodox tradition. Those who articulate the faith need to be formed by tradition and be less given to the shallow and fruitless habit of cribbing from and reacting to non-Orthodox traditions.

At the level of pastoral life, the matter of a renewed understanding of the fathers is again crucial. A return to the fathers is not an escape from the problems of contemporary society since the fundamental theme of patristic theology is *omnia omnibus*, all things to all men. For this reason, only such a return can counteract the heresy of viewing the church as alternative or supplementary to secular society and reveal the full responsibility of her mission to 'make all things new again.' This has everything to do with the Orthodox churches in the diaspora where the church has so far played largely a maintenance role within ethnic groups. In this situation the Orthodox church needs to find a prophetic patristic theology so that it might live anew in the new lands. As one Orthodox theologian recently stated: 'Diaspora is not a curse; potentially it is a blessing! It is not a predicament, ontologically it is an honor! It is not an exile; theologically it is a return to the world: and the "entire" world is the Lord's.'[62]

The Orthodox church faces the double task of articulating an ecclesiology that reflects the diversity of social and political situations in which she now finds herself, such as the diaspora and anti-Christian states (such as under communism and Islam), but the church must also reject pseudo-ecclesiology, which is to say, one based on any person, thing or idea which is not Jesus Christ. The church also faces the immense task of reassessing her structure — patriarchate, diocese or parish — in the light of intense urbanization and depersonalization of modern society. In the same reassessment, the church may need to rediscover the correct role of the monastic life in the church (perhaps Orthodoxy's greatest glory) while at the same time rejecting any notion of the monastery as peripheral to Christian reality on the one hand or as constituting a 'church within a church' on the other.

As for the Catholic church, the twentieth century presents a great challenge to the Orthodox church of the East. The very challenge is an invitation to follow the commands of her divine Master and Spouse, for whom she waits with expectation and joy.

EASTERN RITE CATHOLICS

There are a number of communities of Byzantine Rite Christians who are in communion with the Roman See. Some never really left it, others returned, others were more or less invented by the Roman church. They are most often called 'uniate' churches (those in union). The two largest uniate churches are the Ukrainian Catholics, headed by an Archbishop-Major, and the Melkite church of Antioch, headed by the Catholic Patriarch of Antioch, at present Patriarch Maximos V Hakim. Both churches have communities in most of the major English-speaking countries. Other uniate churches include the Greek church of Sicily and South Italy (a survivor of Byzantine days, also called the Italo-Albanese church), the Ruthenian Catholics and the very tiny Russian Catholic church. The Russian Catholics have a community in Melbourne.

Neither the Roman Catholics, the Orthodox nor historical circumstances have treated these churches very kindly. The Romans have more or less constantly interfered with their customary style of life and with their liturgical traditions; while the Orthodox heartily dislike them, seeing them as dupes of Roman Imperialism, created to lure away the Orthodox faithful to Roman obedience. They have also suffered historical catastrophes such as followed the 1917 revolution in Russia, the Ottoman oppression in the Middle East and exile from their homelands precipitated by World War II. In spite of all, they have continued to exist, adhering to Rome and more or less to their Byzantine traditions.

Despite the latinization of many, there is no question that the Orthodox church is the Mother Church of the Eastern Catholics. Reintegration with her must be their final goal. The task is fearsomely difficult. They must both strive to return to the Mother Church, but without losing communion with Rome. They stand at the very heart of East – West reunion, and given enough charity and courage, the uniates could become the 'Cup in Benjamin's Sack,' drawing the estranged brothers to self-disclosure and reunion. Their existence need not continue to be an unmovable obstacle to unity, but that is the light in which they have been cast up to the present.

Given the state of the uniate churches one could despair of their being equal to the task. There are serious internal divisions, some parties desiring to adhere to the integrity of their Eastern traditions opposing other factions who favor westernization. If the uniate churches are to succeed in their highest purpose, these groups must come to an understanding on a higher level. Providence may intend them to witness to Catholicism and to Orthodoxy, showing both that there is room, in a true unity of Christ's church, for two legitimate expressions of the one faith. Among the Roman Catholics they must defend, to the brink of schism if necessary, the legitimate claims of Eastern theology, church life and spirituality.[63] They must reject all encroachment upon the ancient rights and dignity of the East, such as the celibacy laws. If they fail, the Orthodox will never be convinced that such pressures would not be applied to them in a reunited church.

There are signs of hope. Most Catholics would not realize that one of the sources of Vatican II's new directions in many matters to do with the church, such as the emphasis upon collegiality, came from the East, through the indefatigable efforts of the great Melkite Patriarch, Maximos IV of Antioch, and fellow Eastern Catholic bishops at the council.

TOWARD REUNION

That communion between the churches was lost and is still a goal for the future, is the result of unfortunate historical experiences. That in many cases the churches can barely manage open-

The Patriarchs of Old and New Rome.

countenanced goodwill toward each other, is resistance to the Holy Spirit.

There can be little doubt that the churches of the Catholic tradition — Roman, Orthodox and non-Chalcedonian Orthodox — fundamentally conceive of God, the economy of salvation and God's operation in the world in a consonant way, but historical circumstances forced them apart and denied them the opportunity to appreciate each other's faith. They deepened their ignorance of the cultural milieu which conditioned each sister church's faith and theological outlook. The will to understand was further weakened by the contacts that they did have, such as to establish what was almost an inexorable pattern in their relationships. As mutual ignorance, strangeness and positive misunderstanding deepened, further contact produced only conditioned responses ranging from a lack of will for reunion to an implacable hatred. It is the task of modern ecumenism to break the power of the conditioned response.

To understand why so much of our contemporary endeavors make such little progress must be approached with some understanding of this past. The many memories of unpleasant experiences, as well as more than a thousand years of separation, have imposed upon ecumenical dialogue a diplomatic model. While this model may be suitable for the ordering of the affairs and relationships of nation-states, it is not entirely appropriate as a procedure in the search for the reunion of the church. The use of the diplomatic model reinforces habits, assumptions and reactions which are perhaps inappropriate. It may be that the diplomatic model is incapable of pointing to the features of the kingdom of God. It may well be that it is antipathetical to the kingdom and its ethos, which is an atmosphere conditioned by grace and founded on love. The churches must begin to think and to act, as much as it is possible, as those who already belong together, those whose role is nothing less than the new ordering of the cosmos.

Precisely because the church is the vessel of salvation, truth and the Christian mysteries, reunion recommends itself with particular urgency. In facing the facts of 'the signs of the times' and 'the lateness of the hour,' the churches must appear in their role as the eschatological sign in the world. But as any Christian with some knowledge of ecumenical history knows, unions entered into on the grounds of emergency can create more ecumenical damage than good. Why would anything have changed today when the past shows that unions of this sort (conceived in situations governed by fear) did violence to the truth? Such reservations are serious, but the circumstances of the twentieth century have so altered that these reservations may now have a chance of being satisfied.

The negotiations for reunion between East and West in the late Middle Ages were so colored by politics that the union was almost a forced union. This was the criticism levelled by the faithful laity of the Orthodox at the bishops and emperor after the union of the Council of Florence. It is obvious that the straitened circumstances of the Empire, as well as the possibility of Western assistance, were to the forefront of the negotiators' minds. This is not to charge them with hypocrisy. They doubtless believed in the union. However, it is important to realize that this situation cannot recur in anything like the way it did at the time of the Council of Florence. The chief reason why it cannot recur is to be found in the changed circumstances of all the churches who were either direct participants or represented by some other arrangement. The significant change is that none of these churches any longer identifies itself with the interests, principles or survival of any particular political system or ideology.

In the West, the Catholic church is now an array of local churches whose existence was not dreamed of at Florence. Even the papacy has been finally detached from its place as a quasi-kingdom and secular power among the countries of western Europe. Much the same is true of the East. No thinking churchman or layman among the Greeks would claim that the survival of the church was the same thing as the survival of the State, or that the union of church and State was indispensable as the church's guarantee of survival. Though content to mentally identify Hellenism with Orthodoxy in the everyday functioning of the church, and often much to the annoyance of other Orthodox, the same equation would not be made *in extremis*.

The Catholic church has been forced to rethink its relationship to secular society by the secularist movements and ideologies which sprang from the whole nexus of ideas, dreams, conditions and outcomes surrounding 1789 and the revolution it initiated. Most of the Orthodox churches, in one of those ironical historical situations, were largely untouched. Catholicism took much of the shock. Only echoes of the thunder reached Ottoman Greece, Czarist Russia, the Ottoman territories in Asia Minor, Palestine or Egypt. The equivalent events which have begun to change Orthodoxy came much later and cluster around and proceed from the outcome of events in Russia in 1917.

Both of the great churches are now faced with intellectual, moral and spiritual challenges and issues in a wider world and at a level of complexity not dreamed of even one hundred years ago. The situation of the age makes it doubly urgent that the churches of the East and the Roman church of the West seriously set out to find each other in a situation largely more free of the national interests which once bedeviled the search for union. The sheer scale of the difficulties, dangers, promises and dreams of the twentieth century increases the scandal of Orthodox/Catholic disunity. The whole of Christ's church must speak with a united voice to a planet now in danger of destruction. In the face of such great dangers to mankind, with the specter of secularized Pelagianism standing behind the thinking of the materialist systems of both capitalism and Marxism; in the face of poverty, injustice and the multiplying threats to human life, even from conception; as well as the other host of spiritual needs and ills that plead for Christ's compassion — the rehearsing of offenses and prejudices from a vanished past appears not a little precious to the watching world.

BEGINNING TO UNDERSTAND

What are Catholics faced with when they attempt to seek some form of friendly contact with the Orthodox church? First of all, there is no simple body that is the Orthodox church. If the Orthodox wish to initiate ecumenical contact with Catholics, in say Melbourne or New York, they can approach the body headed by the city's bishop. It does not work like that the other way round. There are many 'jurisdictions' of the Orthodox church. In Australia for example: one Greek, one Antiochian, one Rumanian, two Serbian, one Macedonian,[64] two Ukrainian, two Bulgarian and three Russian. All call themselves Orthodox; all use the same ritual in their services; all have the same ethos, but language, politics and history of computation of the calendar have divided them. We used an Australian example here but the situation is almost identical in the United States and in Canada. There is a plethora of jurisdictions. So where could the Catholic start?

Some jurisdictions would be quite delighted if a Catholic or a group of Catholics attended a service such as the Easter vigil. Others would not be so welcoming, some would be puzzled. In one or two churches a Catholic might even encounter quiet hostility. This is not a very good method of gaining ecumenical contact. This chapter will suggest another method, after it has looked a little more closely at the difficulties. Catholics might be anxious to establish ecumenical contact with Orthodoxy, but are the Orthodox equally desirous of discovering us? Not really. The Orthodox view of Catholicism is still very much conditioned by the past; they still feel the past as present and in the minds of many, clergy and theologians in particular, those past events are still sour in the memory.

Allowing official dialogue between the churches to follow its course among the hierarchies and theologians, the individual, interested Catholic should follow in a different style. It is best to make a friend among the Orthodox. Break the ice with neighbors, at the same time taking the trouble to read something of the doctrinal tradition and history of Orthodoxy. Through your friend and your study you might have a better chance of beginning to understand and to feel something of their feeling. At this point you can venture to a church. Go with your friend. You will not feel anywhere near as awkward and out of place if you begin like this. Go 'under their wing,' so to speak. Let them guide you. Only when steps like this have been taken will the Catholic avoid being a liturgical voyeur or a nuisance. It also seems to be that those who begin by church visiting soon find that their interest wanes once their curiosity has been pandered to. The language of the Eastern services, the distinct style of worship and the devotional attitudes of the East are difficult of access for anyone of the West. Without the friend and serious reading, the Catholic will altogether fail to see the basic unity of belief and practice which, though hidden, link the Catholic and the Orthodox believer.

A little more information on further things that you might encounter may help. In the Russian churches you will find Orthodox worship at its most traditional and observant. The music helps the Catholic to feel a little more at home. It is nearest to the style and singing of the West. Not present-day Catholic popular music, of course. Rather, it is influenced by nineteenth-century German church music. This may be the reason that non-Orthodox most easily 'fall into step' in a Russian church. It is still a little exotic, but not too bizarre and unfamiliar. The Russians, on the other hand, may be none too friendly. The churches of the Patriarchate of Antioch, while almost always open and very friendly to Catholics, present a wildly unfamiliar appearance and sound to the timid visitor. Their liturgical language is Arabic and none too familiar to other Western Christians. Even the Greek style is only slightly less foreign. Superficially the singing is similar to the Arabic singing of the church of Antioch (it is sung in the old Byzantine modes), while the stance of the congregation is a little more ordered and tidy (many Greek churches now have pews), but it is still very strange to an outsider. The Serbian and Macedonian churches — both Slavic churches whose homelands and headquarters are in modern Yugoslavia — are a strange mixture of the dignified and ordered Russian performance of the church services, with more than an echo of the Hellenic neighbors' melodies giving an almost Oriental touch to the way they sing. All these multiple styles, 'various as the human frame, and wondrously made,' have arisen from often tumultous theological and cultural – political history. They are now scattered throughout the suburbs. In the longer term they cannot fail to enrich the new countries.

Since the schism between East and West both sides have suffered from the absence of the other. Both sides limp, as it were. The East lacks something of Western pragmatism, while the West lacks something of their holistic response to the Christian mystery. The East is more Trinitarian in its theological framework. For them the Incarnation flows from that fact. The West is somewhat Christo-centric, with its incarnational response stepping off from the human figure of Jesus Christ. While it is very important not to create a hybrid strain of Oriental and Occidental Christianity, Western Christians stand to gain great insight into the life of the gospel teaching by an open-minded approach to the apostolic Christianity of the Byzantine tradition. The distant scene, which is the possible reuniting of the estranged twins, can be left to God's providence. Worldwide ecumenical activity involving theologians and bishops and perhaps many centuries may bring this about. The local scene is also part of this greater spiritual movement and our relations with neighboring Eastern Christians can help us to see into the full depths of our own tradition while providing a preparation ground for mutual understanding. The new countries, particularly Australia, Canada and the United States, are ideally placed for this work.

The interior of Hagia Sophia, Constantinople.

Conclusion

To look constantly to the past is not to be whole in the present. Never to look to the past is to cast no shadow. Among the churches, the first only creates a bitter sterility. The second creates a church with no mysteries or any compelling beauty. Consequently, the future of the churches can only be founded upon an appreciation of the common Catholic past, admiration for the particular past of each church and a loving attention to each other in the present.

The real causes of the schism are to be found in human failure. Being caused by sins against love, only love can repair and restore the Christian world to visible unity. The search for unity cannot, therefore, be a matter for the conference table or at the level of the hierarchy alone. If this love is not to be abstract, it must arise among the peoples and be both broad and specific. If the Catholic church began to put its heart into serving the East without ulterior motives, treating the Eastern Christians in our midst as brethren with the same rights and inheritance, the response of the Spirit of God would not be slow.

If this book has achieved anything of its purpose it should be clear that the East would not come empty-handed to this agape.

Appendixes

APPENDIX 1:
GENEALOGY OF THE CHRISTIAN LITURGIES

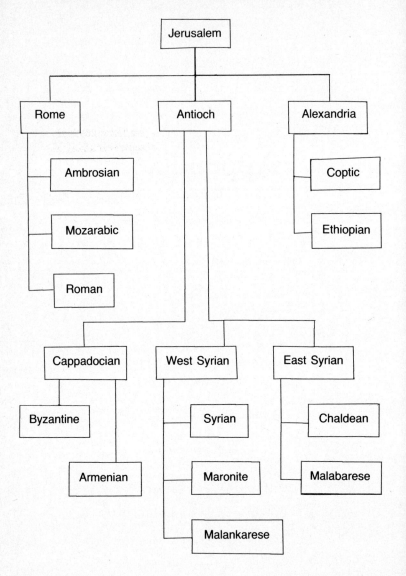

APPENDIX 2:
FURTHER READING

No one has yet written a comprehensive history of the Orthodox church in the English language, but there are some good historical materials in the following.

Attwater, D. *The Christian Churches of the East*, Vol. I, 'Churches in Communion with Rome', and Vol. II, 'Churches not in Communion with Rome' (London: Geoffery Chapman, 1961).

Mayendorff, J. *The Orthodox Church* (New York: St. Vladimir's Seminary Press, 1981). Very readable, the best informed and up-to-date.

Ware, T. *The Orthodox Church* (London: Penguin, 1963). Still a good book but showing its age, particularly in its view of the Western churches.

Six hundred years on, the best introduction to the sacramental and liturgical world of Byzantine Christianity is still that by N. Cabasilas: *A Commentary on the Divine Liturgy* (London: S.P.C.K., 1978).

For the only definitive modern studies in English, of both the liturgy and the sacraments, it is impossible to go past two books by C. Kucharek: *The Byzantine Liturgy of St. John Chrysostom* (Combermere, Ont., Canada: Alleluia Press, 1971), and *The Sacramental Mysteries: A Byzantine Approach* (Combermere, Ont., Canada: Alleluia Press, 1976).

An easy but admirable introduction to the Eastern Christian approach to prayer and the spiritual life can be had in the book by J. Raya: *The Face of God* (Denville, N.J.: Dimension Books, 1976).

One of the most enchanting ways of beginning to understand is to read the Russian pilgrim's story in *The Way of the Pilgrim* and *The Pilgrim Continues His Way*, translated by R.M. French (London: S.P.C.K., 1943 and 1973 respectively).

A fine secondary work is by V. Lossky: *The Mystical Theology of the Eastern Church* (London: James Clarke, 1957).

The deep end of the pool, so to speak, is the rich storehouse of spiritual wisdom known as *Philokalia*, Vols I, II and III, Palmer, Sherrard and Ware, eds (London: Faber, from 1979). The *Philokalia* is the teaching of the great ascetic fathers of the church on the spiritual life and the prayer of the heart.

References

Chapter One HISTORICAL OUTLINES

1. *Contra Celsum*, 111, 28, PE11, 956D.
2. The churches who belong to this grouping are most commonly called monophysite (one nature) churches. The Orthodox most often refer to them as the non-Canonical Orthodox or non-Chalcedonian churches. The Armenian, Ethiopian, Jacobite and Coptic churches belong to this group. Sometimes they are simply called the Oriental churches, which is not very precise.
3. The intellectual and spiritual ancestor of philosophies which see man as perfectible by nature and which deny the Christian belief that man is a fallen being in need of restoration by God.
4. The creation of the dissident Orthodox church, or the non-Chalcedonian Orthodox or the Oriental churches, needs some further explanation. The late Empire was a political and social regime in deep trouble. The deeper the trouble, the more authoritarian did the central government become. Constantine inherited the drift to authoritarianism, problems with labor production and inflation, problems of external security, as well as law and order difficulties with the lower orders of society and racial minorities who felt the hand of authority the heaviest. This is the background to the fifth-century division which occurred in the Eastern Catholic church. The cause of the schism was a question of heresy (the only legitimate cause for suspending communion) but it is also clear that the Syrians and the Copts of Egypt who left communion were also reacting to the oppressive imperial government and to the Greek domination. The causes were clearly mixed ones. Since it was at the Council of Chalcedon that the schism began, unhealed to this day, the Syrians and Copts who formed this movement have been called non-Chalcedonian Orthodox churches, dissident Orthodox churches and, sometimes, Oriental churches.
5. The heresy which takes its name from Arius, a priest of Alexandria, who taught that Jesus Christ was not 'God from true God.'
6. H. Daniel-Rops, *The Church in the Dark Ages* (New York: Image Books, Doubleday, 1962), p. 187.
7. The original Creed of Nicaea – Constantinople states that the Holy Spirit 'proceeds from the Father.' The phrase *filioque* (and from the Son) was first added to the Creed in the Spanish church, perhaps to counteract heresy. Its use was adopted, insisted upon and propagated by Charlemagne and his theologians and was adopted in Rome itself very much later on. The Eastern church strongly objected to its use, saying that it was impertinent to alter the Creed without consiliar authority, and that the phrase, however well intentioned, was not orthodox.
8. V. Lossky, *The Mystical Theology of the Eastern Church* (London: James Clarke, 1957), p. 13.
9. See L. Cross, 'A Clue to the Sources of Schism' in *Chrysostom*, the journal of the Society of St. John Chrysostom, London, 1984.
10. Daniel-Rops, op. cit. p. 262.

11. T. Ware, *The Orthodox Church* (London: Penguin, 1963), p. 69.
12. Ibid., p. 70.

Chapter Two THE BYZANTINE THEOLOGICAL VIEW

13. Nicaea I, 325; Constantinople I, 381; Ephesus, 431; Chalcedon, 451; Constantinople II, 553; Constantinople III, 680; Nicaea II, 787.
14. The two most commonly used forms for private prayer resemble what Catholics would have known as little offices. In the East these are the Acathist Hymn (to Our Lady, to Christ, to a saint or in honor of a mystery of the faith), and the Paraclisis (Consolation). A fervent person would recite these at home before the family icons, with the lamps lit and with an offering of incense.
15. All services, public and private, begin with a prayer to the Holy Spirit. The most common form is: 'O Heavenly King, Consoler and Spirit of Truth, who is in every place and who fills all things; O Treasury of Good and Giver of Life itself, come, take up your abode within us and cleanse us of every stain, and save us O Gracious Lord God.'
16. Joseph M. Raya, *The Face of God* (Denville, N.J.: Dimension Books, 1976), pp. 20–21.
17. Ibid.
18. Ibid., p. 22.
19. The Holy Liturgy, or the Divine Liturgy, is the preferred term used for the Mass by Byzantine Christians.
20. To do with a manifestation of God, a divine manifestation, in the Greek language.
21. To become or turn into God, or more precisely, to be made divine by grace, to participate in God through Jesus Christ the Divine Man.
22. J. Mayendorff, *Byzantine Theology* (London: Mowbrays, 1974), p. 79.
23. H. de Lubac, *Catholicism* (London: Burns and Oates, 1950), p. 4.
24. Ibid., citing *The Roman Catechism*.
25. This is the favorite title for Our Lady in the East. It was given to her at the Council of Ephesus in the fifth century by the whole Christian church.
26. Ephesians 2:19–20.
27. Apocalypse 21:10–14.
28. Raya, op. cit., p. 117.
29. From *omo-phero*, I bear on my shoulders. It represents the lost sheep which the Good Shepherd puts on his shoulders. The lost sheep, of course, is humanity.
30. Bishop Maximos Aghiorgoussis, 'The Parish Presbyter and his Bishop,' *St. Vladimir's Theological Quarterly*, Vol. 29, No. 1, 1985, p. 59.
31. S. Hackel, *The Orthodox Church* (London: Ward Lock Educational, 1974), p. 28.
32. Patriarch Demetrios of Constantinople, Easter Sermon, 1983.

33. A. Khomiakov, in a letter found in W.J. Birkbeck, *Russia and the English Church* (London: 1895), p. 94.
34. Ecumenical in this context means universal in authority and all-embracing in scope.

Chapter Three THE SACRAMENTAL MYSTERIES
35. Homily 56 and Homily 24 on 'St. John' and 1 Corinthians.
36. Pelagius, see reference 3.
37. A. Schmemann, *For the Life of the World* (New York: St. Vladimir's Seminary Press, 1973), p. 89.
38. From the form used by the Melkite church of Antioch, which follows the Greek form.
39. Raya, op. cit., p. 177.
40. St. Nicholas is almost certainly the most popular saint in the Christian East. Inexplicably his feast was demoted in the public calendar of the Roman church in the 1960s, a decision of little ecumenical delicacy.

Chapter Four TRADITION IN LIFE
41. N. Zernov, 'The Eastern Schism and the Eastern Orthodox Church' in R.C. Zaehner (ed.), *Living Faiths* (London: Hutchinson, 1971), p. 86.
42. The preferred terms for 'altar.'
43. Hackel, op. cit., p. 31.
44. In Catholic language, 'sacramentals.'
45. Ware, op. cit., p. 278.
46. Byzantium was the rather sleepy village chosen by the Emperor Constantine as the site for the new capital, Constantinople. Its name is given to describe East Roman civilization as a whole and to describe the marvelously rich synthesis of worship that was forged there and that spread from Byzantium across the Near East and into eastern Europe.
47. Ware, op. cit., p. 272.
48. *Russian Primary Chronicle*.
49. Byzantine Christians make the sign of the Cross with the right hand touching the forehead first, then the right and left shoulders. The Western form is the other way around. They also hold the fingers of their hand differently. The thumb and first two fingers are held together, symbolizing the Holy Trinity; the other two fingers symbolize the divine and human natures of Christ. The Eastern form of the sign of the Cross is the more ancient way of making the sign. The Western manner is a later simplification.
50. St. Gregory Palamas, Patrologia Graeca, 150, 1228.
51. P. Evdokimov, *The Struggle with God* (Glen Rock, N.J.: Paulist Press, 1966), p. 117.
52. From *eschatos* (Greek): last in time, the end times, end of the age. It is interesting that *eschatia*, which is closely related, can also mean a remote retreat, a solitary place, a hermitage.

53. Father Zossima in Dostoevsky's *Brothers Karamazov* is perhaps the most famous literary example of such a figure.
54. Iconoclasts, literally, 'image breakers.'
55. The followers of Mani are the Manichees, a dualist religion founded on a belief in the enmity of spirit and matter which they identified with good and evil. God was identified with all things mental, lofty and spiritual, while the matter of creation and the flesh of man was considered the work of God's evil counterpart.
56. Anointing with oil is a particular sign of creation restored to its true nature in Christ; to its theandric nature, as speaking of God. See Genesis 28:18–19 for the first sign of this in Scripture.
57. D. Ouspensky and V. Lossky, *The Meaning of Icons* (Olten, Switzerland: Urs Graf-Verlag, 1952).
58. Ware, op. cit., pp. 170–171, citing *La Priere de Jesus*, Chevetogne, 1952, and S. Bulgakov, *The Orthodox Church*.
59. Essence must not be thought of as a thing or as a physical substance, rather it is God's being. Consequently, only God knows himself from within, so to speak; that is, essence is God's own knowledge of himself. No creature can aspire to this. However, God can be truly known in his energies, which is to say in what he does and what God does is truly filled with himself. Creatures can participate in God's energies. It is a true communion. In other words, because of the Incarnation, we can truly know God in every way short of being God himself.
60. Translated by R.M. French, London, 1954, and since reprinted.

Chapter Five EASTERN CHRISTIANITY, TODAY AND TOMORROW
61. The fifth Patriarchate is Rome.
62. D.J. Sabas, *Catechesis The Maturation of the Body* (Brookline, Mass.: Holy Cross Orthodox Press, 1984). Reviewed in *St. Vladimir's Theological Quarterly*, Vol. 29, No. 1, 1985, p. 87.
63. Rev. Victor L. Herbeth, 'Uniatism, A Critique,' *Diakonia*, Vol. 2, 1967.
64. The Macedonian Orthodox church, made up of Slavic Macedonians, has not as yet been recognised by any of the other Orthodox churches.